First World War
and Army of Occupation
War Diary
France, Belgium and Germany

14 DIVISION
41 Infantry Brigade
Durham Light Infantry
29th Battalion
19 June 1918 - 30 April 1919

WO95/1895/3

The Naval & Military Press Ltd
www.nmarchive.com
Published in association with The National Archives

Published by

The Naval & Military Press Ltd

Unit 10 Ridgewood Industrial Park,

Uckfield, East Sussex,

TN22 5QE England

Tel: +44 (0) 1825 749494

www.naval-military-press.com

www.nmarchive.com

This diary has been reprinted in facsimile from the original. Any imperfections are inevitably reproduced and the quality may fall short of modern type and cartographic standards.

© Crown Copyright

Images reproduced by permission of The National Archives, London, England, 2015.

Contents

Document type	Place/Title	Date From	Date To
Heading	WO95/1895-3		
Heading	14th Division 41st Infy Bde 29th Bn Durham Lt Infy Jun 1918-Apl 1919 From U.K.		
Heading	War Diary of 29th Bn. Durham Light Infantry From June 19th 1918 To June 30th 1918 Volume I		
War Diary	Brookwood Surrey	19/06/1918	30/06/1918
Heading	War Diary of 29th Battalion Durham Light Infantry From July 1st 1918 To July 31st 1918 Volume II		
War Diary	Brookwood Surrey	01/07/1918	02/07/1918
War Diary	Folkestone	03/07/1918	03/07/1918
War Diary	Boulogne Marquise Fiennes	04/07/1918	04/07/1918
War Diary	Fiennes	05/07/1918	10/07/1918
War Diary	Licques	11/07/1918	11/07/1918
War Diary	Zouafques	12/07/1918	12/07/1918
War Diary	Moulle	13/07/1918	28/07/1918
War Diary	Ebblinghem (Area)	29/07/1918	29/07/1918
War Diary	St. Sylvestre Commune	30/07/1918	31/07/1918
Operation(al) Order(s)	Operation Order No.1 29th Bn Durham Light Infantry	30/06/1918	30/06/1918
Operation(al) Order(s)	Operation Order No.2 29th Bn Durham Light Infantry	09/07/1918	09/07/1918
Operation(al) Order(s)	Operation Order No.3 29th Bn Durham Light Infantry	10/07/1918	10/07/1918
Operation(al) Order(s)	Operation Order No. 4 29th Bn Durham Light Infantry	11/07/1918	11/07/1918
Operation(al) Order(s)	29th Bn Durham Light Infantry Operation Order No. 5	26/07/1918	26/07/1918
Operation(al) Order(s)	29th Bn Durham Light Infantry Operation Order No.6	27/07/1918	27/07/1918
Operation(al) Order(s)	29th Bn Durham Light Infantry Operation Order No. 7	28/07/1918	28/07/1918
Heading	War Diary of 29th Bn Durham Light Infantry From August 1st 1918 To August 31st 1918 Volume III		
War Diary	St Sylvestre Commune	01/08/1918	04/08/1918
War Diary	St. Sylvestre Cappel	05/08/1918	12/08/1918
War Diary	Nieurlet	13/08/1918	13/08/1918
War Diary	Zudrove	14/08/1918	20/08/1918
War Diary	St. Jean. Ter Biezen	21/08/1918	26/08/1918
War Diary	St. Jean. Ter Biezen Brielen	27/08/1918	27/08/1918
War Diary	Ypres	28/08/1918	31/08/1918
Operation(al) Order(s)	29th Bn Durham Light Infantry Operation Order No. 8	11/08/1918	11/08/1918
Operation(al) Order(s)	29th Bn. Durham Light Infantry Operation Order No. 9	12/08/1918	12/08/1918
Operation(al) Order(s)	29th Bn. Durham Light Infantry Operation Order No. 10	19/08/1918	19/08/1918
Operation(al) Order(s)	29th Bn. Durham Light Infantry Operation Order No. 11	27/08/1918	27/08/1918
Operation(al) Order(s)	29th Bn. Durham Light Infantry Operation Order No. 12	28/08/1918	28/08/1918
Heading	War Diary of 29th Battalion Durham Light Infantry From Sept. 1st 1918 To Sept. 30th 1918 Volume IV		
War Diary	Ypres	01/09/1918	05/09/1918
War Diary	Break Camp Sheet 28 G.6.b.	06/09/1918	09/09/1918
War Diary	Brown Line (Arrival Farm)	10/09/1918	12/09/1918
War Diary	Brown Line & Ypres Sector	13/09/1918	13/09/1918
War Diary	Winnizeele	20/09/1918	27/09/1918
War Diary	Reninghelst	27/09/1918	28/09/1918
War Diary	Micmac Camp	29/09/1918	29/09/1918

War Diary	Reninghelst	30/09/1918	30/09/1918
Heading	War Diary of 29th Battalion Durham Light Infantry From October 1st 1918 To October 31st 1918 Volume V		
War Diary	Reninghelst	01/10/1918	01/10/1918
War Diary	Messines	02/10/1918	05/10/1918
War Diary	Messines Area	06/10/1918	08/10/1918
War Diary	Houthem Area	09/10/1918	13/10/1918
War Diary	Comines Area	14/10/1918	15/10/1918
War Diary	Wulverghem	16/10/1918	18/10/1918
War Diary	Comines	19/10/1918	19/10/1918
War Diary	Roncq	20/10/1918	20/10/1918
War Diary	Luingne	21/10/1918	31/10/1918
Operation(al) Order(s)	29th Bn Durham Light Infantry Operation Order No. 20	01/10/1918	01/10/1918
Operation(al) Order(s)	Operation Order No. 21 29th Bn Durham Light Infantry	01/10/1918	01/10/1918
Operation(al) Order(s)	29th Bn Durham Light Infantry Operation Order No. 22	05/10/1918	05/10/1918
Operation(al) Order(s)	29th Bn Durham Light Infantry Operation Order No. 22/A	05/10/1918	05/10/1918
Operation(al) Order(s)	29th Bn Durham Light Infantry Operation Order No. 23	09/10/1918	09/10/1918
Operation(al) Order(s)	29th Bn Durham Light Infantry Operation Order No. 24	13/10/1918	13/10/1918
Miscellaneous	All Coys 29th Durham L.I	14/10/1918	14/10/1918
Miscellaneous	Headquarters 41st Infantry Brigade	17/10/1918	17/10/1918
Operation(al) Order(s)	29th Bn Durham Light Infantry Operation Order No. 26	19/10/1918	19/10/1918
Operation(al) Order(s)	29th Bn Durham Light Infantry Operation Order No. 27	20/10/1918	20/10/1918
Operation(al) Order(s)	29th Bn Durham Light Infantry Operation Order No. 28	31/10/1918	31/10/1918
Operation(al) Order(s)	29th Bn Durham Light Infantry Operation Order No. 13	04/09/1918	04/09/1918
Operation(al) Order(s)	29th Bn Durham Light Infantry Operation Order No. 14	08/09/1918	08/09/1918
Operation(al) Order(s)	29th Bn Durham Light Infantry Operation Order No. 15	12/09/1918	12/09/1918
Operation(al) Order(s)	29th Bn Durham Light Infantry Operation Order No. 16	14/09/1918	14/09/1918
Operation(al) Order(s)	29th Bn Durham Light Infantry Operation Order No. 17	19/09/1918	19/09/1918
Operation(al) Order(s)	29th Bn Durham Light Infantry Operation Order No. 19	27/09/1918	27/09/1918
Heading	War Diary of 29th Battalion The Durham Light Infantry From November 1st 1918 To November 30th 1918 Volume VI		
War Diary	Dottignies	01/11/1918	05/11/1918
War Diary	St Genois Area	06/11/1918	08/11/1918
War Diary	Herseaux	09/11/1918	14/11/1918
War Diary	Bondues Area	15/11/1918	30/11/1918
Operation(al) Order(s)	29th Bn Durham Light Infantry Operation Order No. 29	05/12/1918	05/12/1918
Heading	O C H.Q. Coy		
Operation(al) Order(s)	29th Bn Durham Light Infantry Operation Order No. 30	06/11/1918	06/11/1918
Operation(al) Order(s)	29th Bn Durham Light Infantry Operation Order No. 31	07/11/1918	07/11/1918
Operation(al) Order(s)	29th Bn Durham Light Infantry Operation Order No. 32	08/11/1918	08/11/1918
Operation(al) Order(s)	29th Bn Durham Light Infantry Operation Order No. 33	13/11/1918	13/11/1918
Heading	War Diary of 29th Battalion The Durham Light Infantry From December 1st 1918 To December 31st 1918 Volume VII		
War Diary	Bondues Area	01/12/1918	31/12/1918
Heading	War Diary of 29th Bn Durham Light Infantry From 1st January 1919 To 31st January 1919		
War Diary	Bondues Area	01/01/1919	03/01/1919
War Diary	Tourcoing	04/01/1919	31/01/1919
Heading	War Diary of 29th Bn Durham Light Infantry From 1st February 1919 To 28th February 1919		
War Diary	Tourcoing	01/02/1919	28/02/1919

Operation(al) Order(s)	29th Bn The Durham Light Infantry Operation Order No. 34	02/01/1919	02/01/1919
Heading	War Diary of 29th Durham Light Infantry From 1st March 1919 To 31st March 1919 Volume X		
War Diary	Tourcoing	01/03/1919	31/03/1919
Heading	War Diary of 29th Bn. Durham Light Infantry From-1st April 1919 To-30th April 1919 Volume XI		
War Diary	Tourcoing	01/04/1919	30/04/1919

WO 45/1895 (3)

WO 45/1895 (3)

14TH DIVISION
41ST INFY. BDE

29TH BN DURHAM LT INFY
JUN 1918 - APL 1919

From UK

14-9

Original.   (Copy)

War Diary

of Light Infantry

29th Bn. Durham Light Infantry

from

June 19th 1918 to June 30th 1918.

Volume I

April 19

(Signed:) F.S. Thackeray. Lt. Col.
Cmg. 29th Bn. Durham Light Infantry.

ORIGINAL

Army Form C. 2118.

Instructions regarding War Diaries and Intelligence Summaries are contained in F.S. Regs., Part II. and the Staff Manual respectively. Title pages will be prepared in manuscript.

(COPY).

WAR DIARY
~~INTELLIGENCE~~ SUMMARY

(Erase heading not required.) 29th. Bn. DURHAM LIGHT INFANTRY.

Place	Date	Hour	Summary of Events and Information	Remarks and references to Appendices
Brookwood, Surrey.	19.6.18.		This Battalion was formed. Composition on this date was the Training Cadre of the 2/7 Duke of Wellingtons Regt returned from B.E.F. consisting of 9 Officers and 50 O/Rs, Commanded by Lt. Col. F.S. Thackeray, D.S.O., M.C., (2nd Battn K.L.I.). Draft was received in the afternoon from the West Riding Brigade, representing 4 Regt's, Strength 103 O/Rs. A further draft of 800 men was received about 10.p.m. in the evening. IN this draft the following Regiments were represented. West Yorkshires, Northumberland Fusiliers, Durham L.I. East Yorkshires, K.O.Y.L.I. York & Lancaster, West Riding, East Yorkshire Cyclists. These men were posted to Companies by Regiments. (All men were Cat. B.i. & B.ii.).	WO
"	20.6.18.		A little elementary training was done, men were found to be very backward. Equipping the Battalion for overseas was commenced in the afternoon. Weather to-date was dull and wet.	WO
"	21.6.18.		Little training done. Very busy on equipment, (Web). Men were looking better and taking more interest. A large number by this time had been found to be unfit. An inspection was ordered for Sunday to weed out these unfits.	WO
"	22.6.18.		Training and equiping continued.	WO
"	23.6.18.		All men who had not had draft leave were sent away for four days. No Officers had yet reported for duty, but 4 Officers from 33rd L.R.B. and four from 18th York & Lancasters were attached to us. Battalion was inspected by Reg'tl M.O. of 18th Y & L, with a view to deciding which men should be paraded on Monday as Unfit.	WO
"	24.6.18.		Training on the square carried out with a view to smartening the men up. Specialist Sections were formed and their training commenced. Battalion inspected by a Medical representative of the War Office. 256 presumably unfit men were paraded. Rained all day. Handing in of Home equipment commenced.	WO

O R I G I N A L.

C O P Y

Army Form C. 2118.

WAR DIARY
INTELLIGENCE SUMMARY
of 39th. Bn. DURHAM LIGHT INFANTRY.

(Erase heading not required.)

Instructions regarding War Diaries and Intelligence Summaries are contained in F.S. Regs., Part II and the Staff Manual respectively. Title pages will be prepared in manuscript.

Place	Date	Hour	Summary of Events and Information	Remarks and references to Appendices
BROOKWOOD. Surrey.	25.6.18.		Battalion fired at Century Butts, Bisley. Practices fired:- Application 200 yards, 5 rounds. Rapid 200 yards, 5 rounds. Shooting was good. Lewis Gunners fired at big Siberia Bisley Range. Practice handling gun. Signallers when not firing were instructed by Signalling Officer. Bombers when not firing were instructed by Bombing N.C.O. Stretcher Bearers received instruction under Medical Officer. Special T.M.B. 49 men Grades Unfit. 100 Grade III. A draft of 100 O.Ranks was received from 27 D.L.I. Weather very hot.	Apd.
"	26.6.18.		Following training was carried out:- Gas drill, Musketry, P.T. Squad & Arms Drill, and Specialist Training. Kits were checked and completed. Weather hot.	Apd.
"	27.6.18.		Battalion S.B.Rs. were tested in Gas Chamber at Area Gas School, Blackdown Barracks. A & B Coys fired at Century Butts, Bisley range, practices 200 yards application 10 rounds. 2nd Lt. Smith C.H. appointed Transport Officer. A Draft of 15 Officers was received and posted to Companies.	Apd.
"	28.6.18.		Battalion fired at Century Butts, Bisley Range. Practices application 200 yards 5 rounds with fixed bayonets, rapid 200 yds 5 rounds with S.B.Rs. Baton fired at Big Siberia, Bisley Range, practical handling of Lewis Gun. 9 Officers were received and posted to Coys. Hot weather.	Apd.
"	29.6.18.		Specialist and other training was carried out during the day. Noticeable improvement. 1 Officer reported and was posted to a Coy. Hot weather.	Apd.
"	30.6.18.		Battalion fired at Century Butts, Bisley Range. Squad and Arms drill carried out. No Special 1st Training done. Operation Orders issued regarding Baton proceeding Overseas 1 - 3 July 1918. Hot weather.	Apd.

(Sgd) D.S. THACKRAY, Lieut. Colonel.,
Cdg 39th. Bn. Durham Light Infantry.

Original. 14-9

Vol 2

War Diary

of

29th Battalion Durham Light Infantry.

from

July 1st 1918 to July 31st 1918.

Volume II.

B.W. Ridley   Major.
Cmg. 29th Bn. Durham Light Infantry.

ORIGINAL.

Army Form C. 2118.

WAR DIARY
or
~~INTELLIGENCE SUMMARY.~~
(Erase heading not required.) 29th Battn. DURHAM LIGHT INFANTRY.

Instructions regarding War Diaries and Intelligence Summaries are contained in F. S. Regs., Part II. and the Staff Manual respectively. Title pages will be prepared in manuscript.

Place	Date	Hour	Summary of Events and Information	Remarks and references to Appendices
BROOKWOOD Surrey	1.7.18		Battalion transport entrained at Brookwood Station. Baggage stores &c. also went on train. Capt. W.G. Pagan was in charge of the party. A.T.M.B. available on this day - passed 227 G.R. as unfit for service overseas with the battalion. Firing at Bisley. Siberia, Bisley Range - Lewis Guns, & other practices at Century Butt, Bisley Range. Squad & Arms drill, physical & other training done during the day. Weather hot.	Kent. Operation Order No. 1 appendix to 2.
"	2.7.18		Fitting of equipment & final preparations took place during the day in view of battn. entraining for overseas. All men certified by T.M.B.'s as unfit were passed in the morning ready to move off @ 8 o'clock. Battalion entrained at Brookwood Station for overseas. A & B at 5 & 11.45 p.m. - C & D companies half an hour later. Strength of battalion to entrain. Major P. Bell was detailed as officer i/c stores & Lieut. R. de P. Dallin as officer i/c draft. After the departure of the battn, Lieut. R. de P. Dallin as officer in charge of the 43 rd. overseas any reinforcement to overseas with the draught of the 43 rd. Infantry Brigade. Weather fine but not so hot as day before	Kent.

ORIGINAL.

Army Form C. 2118.

WAR DIARY
or
INTELLIGENCE SUMMARY.

29th Battn. — (Erase heading not required.) DURHAM. LIGHT. INFANTRY.

Instructions regarding War Diaries and Intelligence Summaries are contained in F.S. Regs., Part II. and the Staff Manual respectively. Title pages will be prepared in manuscript.

Place	Date	Hour	Summary of Events and Information	Remarks and references to Appendices
Folkestone	3.7.18		Battalion rested in Folkestone until time for entrainment - 5 a.m. Entrained at Boulogne about 11 a.m. & was marched to Camp "Ostrohove". Here to camp for the night. Men in fairly good spirits. Fine weather.	Lieut.
Boulogne & Marquise & Fienvres	4.7.18	10.30 a.m.	Battalion entrained at Boulogne. — A & B Coys at 7 a.m. B & D Coys at 10.30 a.m. — detrained at Marquise. A, B & D Coy marched to & were billetted in Fienvres, & C Coy at Baucres. The few men to fall out on the march rejoined their companies in about half an hour after destinations reached. Men had their feet inspected. Gales during the afternoon. Major B. W. Bolley M.C. was received as 2nd in command of battalion Capt. J. W. Kaye M.C. & was received as R.C. chaplain. Weather — fine but cool in the morning. Hot in the afternoon.	Lieut.
Fienvres	5.7.18		The Battalion paraded marches under direction of C.C. Companies with the exception of Specialists — Lewis Gun. Bombers, Signallers, Buglers & under specialist officers. Companies had route marches in afternoon in fighting order. R.C. O/o paraded to the excuse under the R.C. M. Walker fine hot.	Lieut.

ORIGINAL

Army Form C. 2118.

WAR DIARY
or
INTELLIGENCE SUMMARY.

(Erase heading not required.) 29th Battn. Durham Light Infantry

Instructions regarding War Diaries and Intelligence Summaries are contained in F. S. Regs., Part II. and the Staff Manual respectively. Title pages will be prepared in manuscript.

Place	Date	Hour	Summary of Events and Information	Remarks and references to Appendices
FIENNES	6.7.18 (Sat)		Squad & Arms drill, route march with fighting order, Specialists training i.e. Lewis Gunners, Signallers, Snipers, Bombers & S.B's. Also Gas drill & Musketry were carried on during the day. 16 O.Rs. under the R.S.M. were paraded in the evening. Weather fine. By this time all Regt. transport has turned up.	Elliot
"	7.7.18 (Sund)		Church services were held during the morning - Church of England in the Village Green, Hardinghen. Roman Catholics at Fiennes. It was noticed that the men marched very well from Fiennes to Hardinghen. No other parades were held during the day & officers though night fine & hot. Weather.	Elliot
"	8.7.18 (Mon)		Battalion was inspected by companies. A Coy was on range from 8.30 a.m. - 12.30 p.m., firing carried out by platoons, the following practices being carried out :- 5 rounds application, 10 rounds rapid. Platoons not firing were trained in Platoon & Coy drill and Visual training. B, C & D Companies carried out during the day; Drill, Bayonet fighting, route march & Specialist training. Gas helmet tests commenced. Weather:- Hot during day - raining at night. Recreational training was done in the afternoon. A special medical board was held by Inspector of drafts & recruits in the E depot, Etaples. 24 O.Rs being sent to the E depot, Etaples.	Elliot

ORIGINAL

Army Form C. 2118.

WAR DIARY
or
INTELLIGENCE SUMMARY.
(Erase heading not required.)

Instructions regarding War Diaries and Intelligence Summaries are contained in F.S. Regs., Part II. and the Staff Manual respectively. Title pages will be prepared in manuscript.

29th Battn. DURHAM LIGHT INFANTRY.

Place	Date	Hour	Summary of Events and Information	Remarks and references to Appendices
FIENNES	9.7.18 (Tues)		During the day the Battalion was employed in Coy drill, bayonet fighting & Specialists training. A.C. & D. Coys Route march in fighting order 9-10.15 a.m. B Coy was on range No. 36 from 8.30 a.m. - 12.30 p.m. Fired the following practices:- 5 rds application, 10 rounds rapid & 5 rounds snap shooting. Pictorial training in afternoon. Brig. General visited battalion. Weather:- Hot.	Nil.
"	10.7.18 (Weds)		Battalion moved from this area to LICQUES. Route taken was as follows:- Alembon, - Eclemy - LICQUES. Billetted for the night. The marching was done fairly well. Weather - Showery. Heavy rain at night. Cool.	Appendix No.3. (Special Order No. 2.)
LICQUES	11.7.18 (Thurs)		Battalion moved from the LICQUES area to ZOUAFQUES. Route taken was:- Courtbourne - Clerques - Guemy - Zouafques, & billetted there for the night. Brigadier General watches Battalion march in. Weather:- fine but cool.	Appendix No. 4. (Operation Order No. 3)
ZOUAFQUES	12.7.18 (Frid)		The Battalion moved from Zouafques to Moulle the final destination in this area. Starting point A.3.75.88 - MOULLE. Battalion marched past the Brig. Gen. into Moulle. Marching considered good. Weather:- Heavy rain throughout the day.	Appendix No. 5. (Special Order No. 4).
MOULLE	13.7.18 (Sat).		Route march by Companies in full marching order. Company drill, bayonet fighting & Specialists training carried out during day. Recreational training in afternoon. Brigade Horse & vehicle after - Fine Baths, wheeled & on foot page	Nil.

ORIGINAL

Army Form C. 2118.

WAR DIARY
or
INTELLIGENCE SUMMARY.
(Erase heading not required.) DURHAM LIGHT INFANTRY
29th Battn

Instructions regarding War Diaries and Intelligence Summaries are contained in F.S. Regs., Part II. and the Staff Manual respectively. Title pages will be prepared in manuscript.

Place	Date	Hour	Summary of Events and Information	Remarks and references to Appendices
MOULLE	14.7.18 (Sun)		Battalion fired on "A" Range as follows:- "A" Coy from 9.30 am to 1 pm. "B" Coy 9.30 a.m. to 1 p.m. "C" Coy 1 p.m. – 4.30 p.m. & "D" Coy 1 p.m. – 4.30. Practices: 5 rounds application at 400x, 10 rounds rapid at 400x & 5 rounds snap shooting at 300x. Dress:- Drill Order. Fine weather.	contd.
"	15.7.18 (Mon)		Battalion marched to training area – the following training carried out during the day:- Specialists, including Lewis Gunners, Snipers, Platoon drill, Gas, handling of arms. Divisional Gas Officer lectured to all officers & N.C.Os. who were transferees to H.Q. & 9th M. Battery, & shook off battalion through. Warmer fine weather.	contd.
"	16.7.18 (Tues)		Battalion on training Area. The following work carried out during day. Specialists training, platoon training, wheeling formation, Extended order, numbering. C.B. Rigby, Commanding Officer, lectured on "Platoon in the Attack". Orders were issued. Shower by day. Thunder storm at night. Orders were received that 2nd Army Commander was to inspect the Battalion on Wednesday 17th	contd.
"	17.7.18 (Wedn)		Battalion was inspected by G.O.C. 2nd Army on the VII Corps Sports Ground, HOULLE. Rained heavily throughout the day. Brigadier called at Battn. orderly room. A draft of 167 O.R.s – part from the 2nd/5th Durham Light Infantry, and from the 3rd K. Royal Fusiliers – was received, posted to Companies.	contd.

ORIGINAL.

Army Form C. 2118.

WAR DIARY
or
~~INTELLIGENCE SUMMARY.~~

(Erase heading not required.) DURHAM. LIGHT. INFANTRY.

29th Battn.

Instructions regarding War Diaries and Intelligence Summaries are contained in F. S. Regs., Part II. and the Staff Manual respectively. Title pages will be prepared in manuscript.

Place	Date	Hour	Summary of Events and Information	Remarks and references to Appendices
Moulle	18.7.18 (Thurs)		Battalion fires on "A" range :- A & B Coys. 8 a.m. - 12 noon, B & D Coys. 12 noon - 4 p.m. Following practices carried out :- 5 rounds application at 300", 10 rds rapid 300", 5 r.d.s. snap shooting 300". P&B specialists also fired. L.G. specialists training.	F.W.T.
"	19.7.18 (Frid)		During the day, Musketry, Physical training, Extended Order drill, & Company in the Attack, were carried out. Also Specialists training. All Lewis Gunners fired on 30 yards range at Q.10.c.1.6 under Lewis Gun Officer. Remainder of Coys (new draft included) under 6.5.N.6.0. weather fine.	F.W.T.
"	20.7.18 (Sat)		Battalion moved to training area in Q.34 - Q.35. "Company in the Attack" was practiced during which all mobilization equipment was carried. Commencing at 9.30 p.m. the practicing of "Relief of Trenches" carried out. It was noticed that all ranks needed more of this work further schemes & time spent would be well spent. Fine during the morning. Heavy rain in afternoon & night.	F.W.T.
"	21.7.18 (Sun)		Voluntary Church parades. Recreation training. Fine weather	F.W.T.
"	22.7.18 (Mon)		Battalion fires on "A" range - Lewis Gunners on 30yds range. Section practices 5 rds application 300", 10 rds rapid 300". S.B.R's @ 300". Most practices required in the latter weather fine. Leaders gave fire orders carried out when men are not firing on range.	F.W.T.

ORIGINAL

Army Form C. 2118.

Instructions regarding War Diaries and Intelligence
Summaries are contained in F. S. Regs., Part II.
and the Staff Manual respectively. Title pages
will be prepared in manuscript.

WAR DIARY
or
INTELLIGENCE SUMMARY.
(Erase heading not required.) DURHAM LIGHT INFANTRY

29th Batt?

Place	Date	Hour	Summary of Events and Information	Remarks and references to Appendices
			2nd Lt A. de Q. Dallen reported with 24 O.R.s. & off strenght in England. Those were posted to Companies.	fwd
MOULLE	23.7.18 (Tues)		Each platoon carried out during the morning "Defence of a strong point", Counter attack to retake strong point" & "Trench relief by day", as a result of inspection by Inspector of Drafts held on 19/7/18. 2 officers & 27 O.Rks - classified below "B.1" - were sent to the Base Depôt Conference rain during morning, finer in afternoon.	fwd
"	24.7.18 (Wed)		Lecture on "Intelligence" was given by Major R.S. Thornton M.C. G.S.O.2 VII Corps. All officers were in attendance. Bgde Sports for Thursday was arranged. Battalion practised during the afternoon "Relief of trenches". A noticeable improvement in the work. Weather fine.	fwd
"	25.7.18 (Thurs)		All platoons were instructed by their own commanders in Troop leading, Use of compass, passing of reports &c., during the morning then appeared been on this work. Brigade Sports were held in afternoon & evening. The Divisional concert party "The Toctows" commenced entertaining in Moville indifferent weather showery at times	fwd
"	26.7.18 (Fri)		Battalion practised by platoons "Defence of Strong Point & Counter-attack to retake". Heavy rain throughout day.	fwd

ORIGINAL

Army Form C. 2118.

Instructions regarding War Diaries and Intelligence Summaries are contained in F. S. Regs., Part II. and the Staff Manual respectively. Title pages will be prepared in manuscript.

WAR DIARY
or
~~INTELLIGENCE SUMMARY.~~
(Erase heading not required.)

29th Battn. DURHAM LIGHT INFANTRY

Place	Date	Hour	Summary of Events and Information	Remarks and references to Appendices
MOULLE	27.7.18 (Sat)		Battalion practised during the day "The Attack" on the training area. Heavy rain throughout day. Reports to move to EBBLINGHEM.	First — appendix to G. (Operation Order No. 5)
"	28.7.18 (Sun)		Battalion marched to the Ebblinghem area. Route taken as follows:— Moulle — St. Omer — Arques — Fortrouge — Renescure — Ebblinghem. Although very tired the men marched very well. Dull but free.	First — appendix to G. (Operation Order No. 6)
EBBLINGHEM (Area)	29.7.18 (Mon)		Battalion moves from this area inward to Camp at P.35.b.5.1. Hot weather.	First — appendix No. 6 (Operation No. 6)
St. Sylvestre CAPPADRE	30.7.18 (Tues)		Except for one platoon & Lewis Gunners of one company who trained for a bit, all men in the Battalion were resting on this opening on a hot day in this area under B.C.'s. A Reveille class was held. All company commanders visited this area in afternoon. Recreational training in afternoon.	First
"	31.7.18 (Wed)		Training work as yesterday. Recreation training. Men appear exceptionally keen enthusiastic over cricket & tennis. Very hot.	First

R.W. Radley Major
LIEUT. COLONEL
CMDG 29 BN. DURHAM L.I.

Copy No. 6
Appendix No. 2

OPERATION ORDER No. 1.
29th. BN. DURHAM LIGHT INFANTRY.

1. The Battalion will proceed overseas commencing Monday July 1st 1918.

2. Entrainment at Brookwood Station will take place as follows:-
   (a) X300 train 7-35.a.m. 1.7.18. The complete transport section to include all attached men plus 6 O.R's from Q.M. Stores Staff. All luggage will proceed on this train except such that can be carried on the man.
   All Officer's valises, stores, and record boxes not required will be stacked at Q.M. Stores by 12 Midnight June 30/July 1st.
   Capt W.C.Pogson will be i/c this party.
   Note:- It must be understood that after this train no further transport for kit will be available.

   (b) X711 train 11-45.p.m. 3/7/18- "A" and "B" Companies.

   (c) X712 train 12-15.a.m. 3/7/18- "C" and "D" Companies. All Regimentally employed men will proceed with their own Companies.

3. A marching-out state will be rendered by Companies to Battalion Orderly Room one hour before the Companies move off.
   Embarkation Rolls will be supplied by Battalion Orderly Room. O.C. half battalions and O.C. Transport section will arrange for their parties to arrive at the Station ½ hours and 3 hours respectively before the train moves off.
   The Officer in charge of Details detailed below will attend the roll-call parade of each party.

4. Major P. Bell is detailed as Officer in charge of Details and after the departure of the Unit will come under the orders of Major W.G. Hayward, Commandant, Stoney Castle Camp. Documents and Nominal Rolls of all men left behind will be handed to him showing how they are situated.

5. Lieut. R.de.F.Dallin is detailed as Officer in charge of Reinforcements.
   He will be given particulars of drafts or men likely to return to the Unit.
   He will proceed overseas in charge of these Drafts with the 43rd Infantry Brigade.

6. A Party of 1 Officer and 50 Other Ranks will be detailed by O.C. D Company to report to the R.T.O. BROOKWOOD at 3.a.m. 1/7/18. They will be employed as loading party for the vehicles.

7. 3 lorries will report to Q.M. at 8-0.a.m. 1/7/18 for conveying baggage to the Station.
   O.C. C Company will detail a party of 1 N.C.O. and 15 men to report to Q.M. at this time to act as Loading Party.

8. C.R.A.C. 57570 (A) D AE92 and 250/14/2 will be read by all O.C. parties, Q.M, T.O, Officer in charge Details at Orderly Room.

H Cameron
Captain & Adjutant.
29th Bn. Durham Light Infantry.

30.6.18.
Issued at 3.30 p.m.
Copies to :- No.1. C.O. No.2. O.C."A" Coy. No.3. O.C. "B" Coy.
No.4. O.C. "C" Coy. No.5. O.C."D" Coy. No.6. 41st Inf Bde
No.7. Q.M. No.8. T.O. No.9. Details.
No.10. War Diary. No.11. File. No.12. R.T.O. Brookwood

J.W. Pepper

SECRET.   Copy No. 10
                                                                          Appendix
O P E R A T I O N   O R D E R No. 2.   No. 3.
29th. BN. DURHAM LIGHT INFANTRY.
....

Ref. Map, Calais 13.

(1) The Battalion will move to-morrow, 10th. instant, from its
     present Area to LICQUES.

(2) Order of march will be :- H.Q.Coy., 'A', 'B', 'D' and 'C'
     Coy.
     (a) 200 yards' distance will be maintained between Companies
         and First Line Transport.
     (b) No smoking except during halts.
     (c) All men falling out will be given a chit by an Officer.
     (d) O.C. 'D' Coy will detail a Guard of 1 Officer and 6 Other
         Ranks to collect Stragglers.
     Bugle Band will parade with 'B' Coy.
     Dress for move :- Marching Order. S.D.Caps will be worn.
     Head of the Column will be at 'A' Coy's Orderly Room at
     8.30 a.m.
     'C' Coy will arrange to join the Column in its correct
     position.
     Transport will follow 'C' Coy.

(3) Route of march will be :- Road junction 200 yards S of D in
     BOUT DES RUES - HERMELINGHEN - Road junction S of 1st O in
     D'ALEMBON - ALEMBON - BOLERY - LICQUES.

(4) Battalion will continue marching on the 11th. instant.

(5) An Advance Party of 1 Officer has already proceeded for
     billeting purposes.
     4 C.Q.M.S's, 1 N.C.O. of H.Q.Coy. (detailed by R.S.M.) and
     1 N.C.O. from Transport Section will leave FIENNES at
     6.30 a.m. on Cycles and report to 2/Lieut.J.C.R.Jeffrey at
     the Church in LICQUES as soon as possible.

(6) Lewis Gun, Bomb and Tool Limbers will be packed to-night and
     parked in Transport Lines.

(7) Quartermaster will send Guide to bring Lorry from 41st.Infantry
     Brigade Headquarters at 8.0 a.m. for carrying surplus stores,etc.

(8) All Officers' Valises, Company Boxes, etc. will be stacked at
     Q.M.Stores by 8.0 a.m.
     O.C. 'C' Coy will arrange for Officers' Valises, Coy Boxes,
     etc. of his Company to be stacked at Coy H.Q. at 7.45 a.m.
     Transport Officer will detail transport to collect these.

Quartermaster will arrange his loading party from his staff.

(9) A Rear Party of 1 Officer and 15 Other Ranks will be detailed by O.C. 'B' Coy.
Clearing Certificates will be obtained by this party from the Area Commandant's Representative.
'C' Coy will arrange their own rear party.

(10) Marching Out States will be at Orderly Room by 8.0 a.m.

(11) Arrival in billets will be reported to Orderly Room immediately.

(12) Rolling Out Returns will be rendered to Orderly Room one hour after arrival in billets.

H Ormerod
Captain & Adjutant,
29th. Bn. Durham Light Infantry.

9.7.19.
Issued at 11.35 p.m.

Copies to :-

No. 1. O.C.'A' Coy.
No. 2. O.C.'B' Coy.
No. 3. O.C.'C' Coy.
No. 4. O.C.'D' Coy.
No. 5. 41st. Infantry Brigade.
No. 6. T.O.
No. 7. Q.M.
No. 8. Officer i/c Stragglers.
No. 9. Area Commandant, WARRINGTON.
No.10. War Diary.
No.11. File.

SECRET.   Copy No...11...

OPERATION ORDER No.3.
29th. BN. DURHAM LIGHT INFANTRY.

Appendix No.4

Ref. Map, CALAIS 13.
 "   " HAZEBROUCK 5.A.

(1) The Battalion will move to-morrow, 11th. instant, from its present Area to ZOUAFQUES.

(2) Reveille 4.30 a.m.
    Breakfast 5.30 a.m.
    Order of march will be :- H.Q.Coy., 'A', 'B', 'C' and 'D' Coy.
    (a) 200 yards' distance will be maintained between Companies and First Line Transport.
    (b) No smoking except during halts.
    (c) All men falling out will be given a chit by an Officer.
    (d) O.C. 'A' Coy will detail a Guard of 1 Officer and 6 Other Ranks to collect Stragglers.
    (e) All transport personnel will wear full marching order (drivers will not wear packs).
    (f) One cook will march behind each "Cooker". The remaining personnel attached to the transport will march as a formed party in rear of the transport.
    Bugle Band will parade with 'C' Coy.
    <u>Dress for move</u> :- Marching Order. S.D.Caps will be worn.
    Head of the Column will be at Point F.3.45.48. at 8.30 a.m.
    Transport will follow 'D' Coy.

(3) Watches will be synchronised at Battalion Orderly Room at 7.0 a.m.

(4) Supply arrangements will be as follows :-
    11th. July - Refilling will take place at TOURNEHEM Church at 7 p.m. for consumption 13th.
    12th. July - Refilling will take place at MOULLE Church at 7 p.m. for consumption 14th.
    Supply Wagons will draw and deliver to Unit on both dates.

(5) Railhead from 13th. July will be at WATTEN.

(6) Route of march will be :- LICQUES - COURTBOURNE - CLERQUES - GUEMY - ZOUAFQUES.

(7) Battalion will continue marching on the 12th. instant.

(8) An Advance Party of 1 Officer and 5 Other Ranks has already proceeded for billeting purposes.
    Os. C. Companies will have either C.Q.M.S. or N.C.O. ready to proceed within ½ hour of arrival in billets as billeting

1.

party for new Area.

(9) Lewis Gun, Bomb and Tool Limbers will be packed to-night and parked in Transport Lines.

(10) Transport Officer will arrange to collect stores from H.Q. Mess and Orderly Room and deliver to Q.M.Stores.

(11) All Officers' Valises, Company Boxes, etc. will be stacked at Q.M.Stores or H.Q.Mess by 7.15 a.m.
O.C.'C' Coy will arrange for Officers' Valises, Company Boxes, etc. of his Company to be stacked at Company H.Q. at 7.0 a.m.
Transport Officer will detail transport to collect these.
Quartermaster will arrange his loading party from his staff.

(12) A Rear Party of 1 Officer and 15 Other Ranks will be detailed by O.C.'D' Coy.
1 N.C.O. from each Company will report to the Officer detailed to point out the billets occupied by his Company.
Clearing Certificates will be obtained by this party from the Area Commandant's Representative.

(13) Marching Out States will be at Orderly Room by 7.30 a.m.

(14) Arrival in billets will be reported to Orderly Room immediately.
Billeting Returns as per pro-forma circulated to-day will be rendered to Orderly Room 6 hours after arrival in billets.

(15) Falling Out Returns will be rendered to Orderly Room one hour after arrival in billets.

Captain & Adjutant,
20th. Bn. Durham Light Infantry.

10.7.18.
Issued at :
Copies to :-

No. 1. O.C.'A' Coy.
No. 2. O.C.'B' Coy.
No. 3. O.C.'C' Coy.
No. 4. O.C.'D' Coy.
No. 5. 41st. Infantry Brigade.
No. 6. T.O.
No. 7. Q.M.
No. 8. Officer i/c Stragglers.
No. 9. Area Commandant, LICQUES.
No.10. War Diary.
No.11. File.

SECRET.   Copy No. 9

OPERATION ORDER No. 4.
29th. BN. DURHAM LIGHT INFANTRY.

Appendix No. 5.

Ref. Map HAZEBROUCK 5.A.

(1) The Battalion will move to-morrow, 12th. instant, from its present Area to MOULLE.

(2) Reveille 4.30 a.m.
Breakfast 5.30 a.m.
Order of march will be :- H.Q.Coy., 'A', 'B', 'C' and 'D' Coy.
  (a) 200 yards' distance will be maintained between Companies and First Line Transport.
  (b) No smoking except during halts.
  (c) All men falling out will be given a chit by an Officer.
  (d) O.C. 'B' Coy will detail a Guard of 1 Officer and 6 Other Ranks to collect Stragglers.
  (e) All transport personnel will wear full marching order. (drivers will not wear packs).
  (f) One cook will march behind each "Cooker". The remaining personnel attached to the transport will march as a formed party in rear of the transport.
Bugle Band will parade with 'D' Coy.
<u>Dress for move</u> :- Marching Order. S.D. Caps will be worn.
Head of the Column will be at Cross-roads A.3.75.88. at 8.0 a.m.
Transport will follow 'D' Coy.

(3) Watches will be synchronised at Battalion Orderly Room at 7.0 a.m.

(4) Route of march will be :- Cross-roads A.3.75.88. - MOULLE.

(5) MOULLE will be the final destination of the Battalion in this Area.

(6) An Advance Party of 1 Officer and 5 Other Ranks has already proceeded for billeting purposes.

(7) Lewis Gun, Bomb and Tool Limbers will remain packed to-night and parked in Transport Lines.

(8) All Officers' Valises, Company Boxes, etc. will be stacked at Q.M. Stores by 7.15 a.m.
Quartermaster will arrange his loading party from his staff. The 5 G.S. Wagons will remain with the Unit until completion of move to-morrow and will then rejoin S.A.A. Section, D.A.C. Supply and Baggage Wagons will rejoin No. 2. Coy, Divisional Train by 6 p.m. on 13th. instant.

1.

(9) A Rear Party of 1 Officer and 15 Other Ranks will be
    detailed by O.C. 'C' Coy.
    1 N.C.O. from each Company will report to the Officer
    detailed to point out the billets occupied by his Company.
    Clearing Certificates will be obtained by this party from
    the Area Commandant's Representative.

(10) Marching Out States will be at Orderly Room by 7.30 a.m.

(11) Arrival in billets will be reported to Orderly Room
     immediately.
     Billeting Returns as per pro-forma already circulated will
     be rendered to Orderly Room 6 hours after arrival in
     billets.

(12) Falling Out Returns will be rendered to Orderly Room one
     hour after arrival in billets.

H Emmerson
Captain & Adjutant,
29th. Bn. Durham Light Infantry.

11.7.18.
Issued at 2.45 p.m.
Copies to :-

No. 1. O.C. 'A' Coy.
No. 2. O.C. 'B' Coy.
No. 3. O.C. 'C' Coy.
No. 4. O.C. 'D' Coy.
No. 5. 41st. Infantry Brigade.
No. 6. T.O.
No. 7. Q.M.
No. 8. Officer i/c Stragglers.
No. 9. War Diary.
No.10. File.
No.11. Area Commandant.

<u>SECRET</u>.　　　　　　　　　　　　　　　　　　　Copy No. 17.

29th. Bn. DURHAM LIGHT INFANTRY.

<u>OPERATION ORDER. NO 5.</u>　　Appendix No. 6

Ref Map 27.

(1). The Battalion will relieve the 33rd. London Regt., on Sunday, July 28th, in the WINNIZEELE DETACHMENT.

(2). The Battalion will proceed to new Area by Lorry.
Companies will form up in fours with head of the column at Battalion Headquarters at 9.0.a.m.
6 Lorries will be allotted to each Company including Headquarters Company.
2/Lieut. F.G.W. Pepper., M.C. will be in charge of embussing.
<u>Dress</u>:-　Marching Order, Caps S.D.

(3). Transport will proceed by road staying for one night 28/29th. instant at NOORDPEENE.
Transport Officer will send forward mounted N.C.O. to arrange billets with Area Commandant.
One N.C.O. from Transport will accompany Headquarters by Lorry to arrange billets at final destination.

(4). Guides for each Company will be sent by 33rd. London Regt to P.35.d.3.5.

(5). Each man will carry rations for consumption on 28th inst.
Rations for 29th inst. will be transported in bulk by the Quartermaster. (less those of Transport Section).

(6). All Maps and Papers referring to work and Defence Schemes will be taken over.

(7). All Lewis Gun Limbers, etc., will be packed on the evening of 27th inst. and parked at Transport Lines.

(8). Blankets, Surplus stores, Officers' Valises, Mess Kits, Cooking utensils for one day etc., will be stacked at Quartermaster's Stores by 8.0.a.m.
Blankets will be securely rolled in bundles of 10 and clearly marked.
4 Lorries will report to Quartermaster for transport of these stores.

(9). Weather permitting, Companies will be clear of billets by 8.0.a.m.
A Representative of the Area Commandant will inspect billets.
2/Lieut.G.Hattersley will obtain clearing certificates in triplicate.

(10). Os.C. Companies, O.C. Headquarters Company, Transport Officer and Quartermaster will render Certificate that all claims preferred against them by owners of billets have been settled.
The Interpreter will obtain a "Certificat de bien vivre" from the owner of each billet, vacated by this Unit.
Pro-formas can be obtained from Orderly Room.

(11). ACKNOWLEDGE.

　　　　　　　　　　　　　　　　　H Ormerod
　　　　　　　　　　　　　　　　　Captain & Adjutant.
　　　　　　　　　　　　　　　　　29th. Bn. Durham Light Infantry.

26.7.18.
Issued at 10.45 /p.m.
Copies to :-

No. 1. C.O.	No. 8. 33rd.L.Rgt.	No.15. M.O.
No. 2. O.C.'A' Coy.	No. 9. T.O.	No.16. Interpreter.
No. 3. O.C.'B' "	No.10. Q.M.	No.17. War Diary.
No. 4. O.C.'C' "	No.11. 2Lt.G.Hattersley.	No.18. File.
No. 5. O.C.'D' "	No.12. 2Lt.F.G.W.Pepper.M.C.	
No. 6. 41st. I.B.	No.13. O.C. Signals.	
No. 7. 18th Y & L.	No.14. Area Commandant.	

MOULLE.

SECRET.   Copy No. 19.

29th. Bn. DURHAM LIGHT INFANTRY.

OPERATION ORDER No. 6.

Appendix No. 7

Ref Map 27.
Operation Order No 5 is cancelled.

1. The Battalion will proceed by route march to EBBLINGHEM to-morrow the 28th instant.

2. Order of march will be :- H.Q. Coy., 'A' Coy, 'B' Coy, 'C' and 'D' Coy.
    (a). 200 yards distance will be maintained between Companies and First Line Transport.
    (b). No smoking except during halts.
    (c). All men falling out will be given a chit by an Officer.
    (d). O.C. 'B' Coy will detail a Guard of 1 Officer and 6 Other Ranks to collect Stragglers.
   Bugle Band will parade with 'A' Coy.
   Dress:- Marching Order, Caps S.D.
   Head of the Column will be at Battalion Headquarters at 9.a.m.
   Companies will form up in column of route facing South East.
   Transport will follow 'D' Coy.

3. Route of march will be :- MOULLE - ST OMER - ARQUES - FORTROUGE - REMESCURE - EBBLINGHEM.

4. Battalion will continue marching on the 29th. instant.

5. Advance Party of 2/Lieut. F.G.W.Pepper, M.C. C.Q.M.S's, and 1 N.C.O. each for Transport and H.Q. Coy will proceed on cycles leaving Headquarters at 8.a.m.
   O.C. Signals will arrange Cycles.

6. All Lewis Gun Limbers, etc. will be packed to-night and parked in Transport Lines.

7. Blankets, surplus stores, Officers' Valises, Mess Kits etc, will be stacked at Quartermaster's Stores by 8.a.m.
   Blankets will be securely rolled in bundles of 10 and clearly marked. labelled.
   3 Motor Lorries and 2 Baggage Wagons will report to Quartermaster for transport of these stores. The 3 Motor Lorries will proceed direct to final destination.
   Quartermaster will arrange loading party from his staff.

8. A rear party consisting of 2/Lieut .G. Hattersley and 5 men per Coy will remain behind.
   These men will know the billets of their Coy.
   A Representative of the Area Commandant will inspect billets at 8.a.m
   2/Lieut.G.Hattersley will obtain clearing certificates in triplicate.

9. Marching Out States will be rendered to Orderly Room by 8.a.m.

10. Arrival in billets will be reported to Orderly Room immediately.

11. Falling Out Returns will be rendered to Orderly Room 1 hour after arrival in billets.

1.

12. Os.C. Companies, O.C. Headquarters Coy, Transport Officer and Quartermaster will render Certificate that all claims preferred against them by owners of billets have been settled. The Interpreter will obtain a "Certificat de bien-vivre" from the owner of each billet vacated by this Unit.
Pro-formas can be obtained from Orderly Room.

13. ACKNOWLEDGE.

H. Comewick
Captain & Adjutant,
29th. Bn. Durham Light Infantry.

27.7.18.
Issued at 8 pm
Copies to:-
No. 1. C.O.
No. 2. O.C. 'A' Coy.
No. 3. O.C. 'B' "
No. 4. O.C. 'C' "
No. 5. O.C. 'D' "
No. 6. Q1st. I.B.
No. 7. 18th. Y. & L.
No. 8. 33rd. L.Rgt.
No. 9. T.O.
No.10. Q.M.
No.11. 2/Lt.G.Hattersley.
No.12. 2/Lt.F.G.W.Pepper.M.C.
No.13. O.C.Signals.
No.14. Area Commandant, MOULLE.
No.15. M.O.
No.16. Interpreter.
No.17. O i/c Stragglers.
No.18. War Diary.
No.19. File.

S E C R E T. 29th. Bn. DURHAM LIGHT INFANTRY.

Copy. No. 16

OPERATION ORDER. NO. 7.

Appendix No. 8

Ref Map 27.

(1) The Battalion will proceed by route march to Camp at P.35.b.5.1. to-morrow, 29th. instant.

(2) Order of march will be :- H.Q.Coy, 'A', 'B', 'C' and 'D' Coy.
    (a) 200 yards' distance will be maintained between Companies and First Line Transport.
    (b) No smoking except during halts.
    (c) All men falling out will be given a chit by an Officer.
    (d) O.C.'C' Coy will detail a Guard of 1 Officer and 6 Other Ranks to collect Stragglers.
Bugle Band will parade with 'B' Coy.
Dress:- Marching Order, S.D.Caps.
Head of the Column will pass Starting Point at 9-30.a.m.
Starting Point will be Road Junction U.9.6.7.6

(3) Route of march will be :- STAPLE - LE BREARDE - P.35.b.5.1.

(4) Advance Party of 2/Lieut N.J. Marsh and 2.N.C.O's from H.Q. will proceed on cycles leaving Headquarters at 7.0.a.m.
O.C. Signals will arrange Cycles.

(5) All Lewis Gun Limbers, etc, will remain packed to-night and parked in Transport Lines.

(6) Quartermaster will arrange to collect Mess Boxes, Stores. etc. from Companies and Headquarters by 8-30.a.m.
He will arrange loading party from his staff.

(7) A rear party consisting of 2/Lieut F.G.W, Pepper. M.C. and 5 men per Company will remain behind.
These men will know the billets of their Company.
A Representative of the Area Commandant will inspect billets at 9-0.a.m.
2/Lieut. F.G.W. Pepper, M.C. will obtain Clearing Certificate in triplicate.

(8) Marching Out States will be rendered to Orderly Room by 8-0.a.m.

(9) Arrival in billets will be reported to Orderly Room immediately.

(10) Falling Out Returns will be rendered to Orderly Room 1 hour after arrival in billets.

(11) ACKNOWLEDGE.

                        Captain & Adjutant,
                      29th. Bn. Durham Light Infantry.

28.7.18.
Issued at 10 p.m.
Copies to :-
No. 1. C.O.
No. 2. O.C. 'A' Coy.
No. 3. O.C. 'B' "
No. 4. O.C. 'C' "
No. 5. O.C. 'D' "
No. 6. 41st. I.B.
No. 7. 33rd. L. Rgt.
No. 8. T.O.
No. 9. Q.M.
No. 10. O.C. H.Q. Coy.
No. 11. 2/Lt.F.G.W.Pepper.M.C.
No. 12. O.C. Signals.
No. 13. Area Commandant, RENESCURE.
No. 14½. M.O.
No. 15. O. i/C Stragglers.
No. 16. War Diary.
No. 17. File.

Original

WK 3

War Diary

of

29th Bn. Durham Light Infantry

from

August 1st. 1918 to August 31st. 1918.

Volume III.

W. Ridley   Major.
Comdg. 29th. Bn. Durham Light Infantry.

Original

Army Form C. 2118.

WAR DIARY
INTELLIGENCE SUMMARY

29th Battn. DURHAM LIGHT INFANTRY

Place	Date	Hour	Summary of Events and Information	Remarks and references to Appendices
St. Sylvestre Cappel Commune	1.8.18. (Thurs)		Lewis Gunners of "D" Coy - the 4 platoon remained in camp for training - remainder of the Battalion digging trenches in the area under R.E. Engineers. Recreational training took place in the afternoon - football v. cricket being the chief games. Hot weather.	first
Do	2.8.18. (Frid)		All Battalion working under R.E.'s. Coy. Lewis Gunners of "B" Coy & No 2 Platoon for training. 1 Officer proceeded on leave. Recreational training - football v. cricket - was played during the afternoon & evening. Hot weather.	first
Do	3.8.18. (Sat)		Lewis Gunners of "B" Coy & No 2 Platoon firing at 30 yards range at V36.50.85. was used by No. 2 Platoon. Remainder of battalion trench digging &c. in this area. Recreational training was carried out during the day. There were very keen & enthusiastic inter Coy. matches.	first
Do	4.8.18. (Sun)		The Commanding Officer (Major Berkeley M.C.) inspected the whole Battalion (except Roman Catholics) in the morning. A aforesaid satisfaction at the good turn out of the men & urged them to make great efforts to eventually become the best battalion - physically & morally - in their Brigade. There paraded by the words of the C.O. Service for R.C.'s was held in Church at St Sylvestre Cappel. Sport was played in the afternoon & evening.	first

D.D. & L. London, E.C.

Original

Army Form C. 2118.

WAR DIARY
or
INTELLIGENCE SUMMARY

(Erase heading not required.) DURHAM LIGHT INFANTRY — 20th Battn

Army Form C. 2118.

Place	Date	Hour	Summary of Events and Information	Remarks and references to Appendices
ST. SYLVESTRE CAPPEL	5.8.18 (Mon)		Bn. of Battalion talks at BAVINCHOVE. About 103 Officers & Other ranks were detailed for work under R.E. Horse shows. Parties were sent for this purpose. The Battalion was awarded 3rd prize for the best turned out entered wagon & pair of light Draft horses. 7 men reported for duty with the Transport. Fine hot weather. Hourly "Roll for all N.C.O.s commenced.	Lieut.
Do.	6.8.18 (Tues)		Battalion carried out the following during the day:- No.10 platoon remained in camp for training. Lewis Gunners of "B" Coy fires on the 30 yards range at V.3.b.50.85. Details talks at BAVINCHOVE. H.M. King George V. accompanied by several Generals visited the area. Coopery classes commenced. Fine weather.	Lieut.
Do.	7.8.18 (Wed)		Lewis Gunners of "A" Coy fires on range at V.3.b.50.65. No.14 platoon remained in camp for training. Special Order of the day by F.M. Sir Douglas Haig, was read out to the Battalion. This was in connection with 4th anniversary of the 4th year of war. A platoon, under 2nd/Lt Lockwood, proceeded on Bridge Guarding. Battalion held its first concert which proved successful. Fine weather. Except for Lewis Gunners of "B" Coy & No.14 platoon which remained	Lieut.
Do.	8.8.18 (Thurs)		in camp for training. The Battalion was digging &c on the Trench systems in the area. As a result of a Medical Board one Officer was transferred to the Base. Exhibition training 150th platoon	Lieut.

Original

Army Form C. 2118.

WAR DIARY
or
~~INTELLIGENCE SUMMARY.~~

(Erase heading not required.) DURHAM LIGHT INFANTRY —
— 29th Battn.

Instructions regarding War Diaries and Intelligence Summaries are contained in F. S. Regs., Part II. and the Staff Manual respectively. Title pages will be prepared in manuscript.

Place	Date	Hour	Summary of Events and Information	Remarks and references to Appendices
ST. SYLVESTRE CAPPEL	9.8.18 (Fri)		Lewis Gunners of B. Coy. on range at V5 b 50.85 - Nos 114 Platoon remained in camp for training. Platoon Selection training. Recreational sport afternoon arrival. Lt. Col. Thackeray (acting Brig. Gen.) worked Battn.	Fine Wet
Do.	10.8.18 (Sat)		Nos 1 of the Battalion worked on trench system in area. Nos 1 to 7 Platoon training in camp. - Lewis Gunner of "D" Coy. Sports were carried out during the afternoon. Weather fine	Fine Wet
Do.	11.8.18 (Sun)		Work as yesterday carried out. Battalion also prepared to move from this area. Men were benefitted considerably by Recreational training whilst in this area. Fine weather	Fine Wet
Do.	12.8.18 (Mon)		Battalion entrained at STEENVOORDE — detrained at ST. MOMELIN. Route to Station Camp. St. Sylvestre Cappel, Waegebrugge, Wagenbrugge & Steenvoorde. Two other ranks met with an accident en route. After detraining at St. Momelin Battalion marched to NIEURLET were billeting was done for the night. Fine fine weather. Transport proceeded by road.	Fine Wet Speeches Order No. 8 appendix No. 9
NIEURLET	13.8.18 (Tues)		Battalion marched from this area to ZUDROVE. Route taken was as follows:— Nieurlet, Le Bas, Serques & Zudrove. Men marched very well no one falling out. Fine shot. Weather	Speeches Order No. 9 appendix No. 10
ZUDROVE	14.8.18 (Wedn)		All Coys. Acpt. H.Q. Coy. & Transport action ballon at LE MARAIS. The M.O. talked to the men after ballon. Many of the Officers were umpires at ~~Rope~~ field day. Fine weather	Fine Wet

Original

Army Form C. 2118.

WAR DIARY
or
INTELLIGENCE SUMMARY

(Erase heading not required.) 29th Battn. DURHAM·LIGHT·INFANTRY –

Instructions regarding War Diaries and Intelligence Summaries are contained in F. S. Regs., Part II. and the Staff Manual respectively. Title pages will be prepared in manuscript.

Place	Date	Hour	Summary of Events and Information	Remarks and references to Appendices
ZUDROVE	16.8.18 (Thurs)		Companies paraded under C.C. Coy's arrangements. Major Ridley (Commanding Officer) nues "Notes on training" in accordance with General Thoro. conference, the pamphlet "Hints on training". C.C. held a conference with Company Commanders. To Bn. Coy. transport later to Lieut. Col. Thackray D.S.O. M.C (Actg. Brigadier General 4th N.B.) visited Battalion. Senior Officers were taken a ride by the Byse Transport Officer. Major General Senner visited the Transport lines. Fine weather.	Gent
Do.	16.8.18 (Frid)		Battalion paraded was instructed in various subjects by platoon Commanders & section leaders. Battalion drill for an hour after that C.C. (Major Ridley M.C.) spoke to the men afterwards to all Officers & N.C.O's. Recreational training in afternoon. Classes in Lewis Gun, Gas, Bombing & Musketry.	Gent
Do.	17.8.18 (Sat)		Training as for the 16.8.18 was carried out during day. Officers R.C. Co. derives and benefit from the various classes held. Alfreg Service (Rev Col. Thackray) visited Battalion. Wooden training order ready to move from this place issued. Fine weather.	Gent
Do.	18.8.18 (Sun)		Divine services for all denominations were held during the day. Three Officers are placed in the charge of the Battalion Stores to be ready to move from this place issued.	Gent

Army Form C. 2118.

Original

WAR DIARY
or
INTELLIGENCE SUMMARY.
(Erase heading not required.) 29th Battn. DURHAM LIGHT INFANTRY

Instructions regarding War Diaries and Intelligence Summaries are contained in F.S. Regs., Part II. and the Staff Manual respectively. Title pages will be prepared in manuscript.

Place	Date	Hour	Summary of Events and Information	Remarks and references to Appendices
ZUDROVE	19.8.18 (Mon)		Companies trained under own arrangements various subjects were dealt with during the day. Officers & N.C.O.s paraded for instruction in Lewis Gun Bombing, Gas & Musketry. Battalion was ready to move from this area to St. Jean·Ter·Biezen.	Appx.
Do.	20.8.18 (Tues)		The Battalion entrained at WATTEN to PROVEN & marched to Road Camp Sheet 27 F.25.A.7.2. Portion of transport proceeded by rail via St. Omar, the remainder by road. A/Bgdr Guvre (Lt. Col. Thackeray) saw all Brigade entrained. Fine weather.	Appx. Garden G. No. 10 Appendix No. 11.
St. JEAN·TER· BIEZEN	21.8.18 (Wedn)		Battalion continued to train in this area. New own programmes & N.C.O. Classes were responsible for Officers & N.C.O.s classes held on numerous subjects. Fine 6 R.R.s proceeded to Base as a result of Medical Board.	Appx.
Do.	22.8.18 (Thurs)		The following morning was carried out during the day:- Gas drill, Wire-communication & orders. Battalion drill ee. Lecture Co-operation of Infantry with Tanks was given by Lt. Col. F.B. Thackeray, D.S.O. M.C. During the night a route march & Outpost scheme was carried out in about TEAK WOOD F.26.a.70.55. Live Grenades were also thrown fine day.	Appx.
Do.	23.8.18 (Frid)		Battalion was allotted billets. Men companies not taking part in afternoon carried a variety of training May Recreational training in afternoon. Good weather shown in football matches Officers & N.C.O.s above, tele in afternoon of the Brigade. Fine day.	Appx.

Original

Army Form C. 2118.

WAR DIARY
or
INTELLIGENCE SUMMARY.
(Erase heading not required.) DURHAM · LIGHT · INFANTRY
— 29th Battn —

Instructions regarding War Diaries and Intelligence Summaries are contained in F. S. Regs., Part II. and the Staff Manual respectively. Title pages will be prepared in manuscript.

Place	Date	Hour	Summary of Events and Information	Remarks and references to Appendices
ST. JAN-TER-BIEZEN.	24-8-18 (Sat)		Battalion carried out training under Coy arrangements were taken. Drill, Gas, Lewis Gun &c. Unit Commanders, Scouts Officers attended in our lines & supervision followed as to training of Scouts Observers &c. Brigadier General was present. 30 yards range near camp was used by Snipers. Recreational training in afternoon evening. Fine dry weather.	Lieut
Do.	25-8-18 (Sun)		During the morning Divine Services were held for all Denominations. Inter Coy & Battalion football matches were played during the day. During the evening fine weather. Heavy rain.	Lieut
Do.	26-8-18 (Mon)		Heavy rain fell during the day. In consequence very little outdoor training was carried. Lectures by Platoon Commanders were given. Warning order issued regarding Battalion's move into Reserve Area. Recreation Sport in evening.	Lieut
Do. & BRIELEN	27-8-18 (Tues)		Battalion proceeded by train from LANCASTER Stn. F.19.c.5.7 (Sheet 28) to MISSION JUNCTION B.27.d.0.2 (Sheet 28). Relieved 1/4th Cheshire Regt. in Brigade Reserve. Transport proceeded by road via POPERINGHE to destination A.30.d. Battn. Hd. Qrs at B.28.d.6.4. Dull & showery.	Lieut Garston taken to " Appendix No. 12.

Army Form C. 2118.

Original

WAR DIARY
or
INTELLIGENCE SUMMARY.

(Erase heading not required.) DURHAM LIGHT INFANTRY —
— 29th Battn

Instructions regarding War Diaries and Intelligence Summaries are contained in F.S. Regs., Part II. and the Staff Manual respectively. Title pages will be prepared in manuscript.

Place	Date	Hour	Summary of Events and Information	Remarks and references to Appendices
BRIELEN & YPRES	28.8.18 (Weds)		Lieut Colonel Mackay, D.S.O. M.C. relinquished the command of this unit & proceeded to join his own battalion, the 2nd Gordon Highland Light Infantry to assume command of the same. Major B.W. Ridley M.C. assumes command of this unit. The Battalion relieved the 5th Bn. K.O.S.B in Brigade Reserve in YPRES. Bn.H.Q. in Ramparts I.8.a.03.76 (Sheet 28 N.W). During the evening, heavy rain. Fine rest of the day.	See Operation Order No. 12 Appendix No. 13
YPRES	29.8.18 (Thurs)		Working parties were found & work commenced under supervision of R.E. in locality. B.G.C. visited all lines. Fine weather. G.O.C. in locality	See P
Do.	30.8.18 (Frid)		Two Coys. bathing. Works under R.E. carried out as yesterday. Fine but dull.	See P
Do.	31.8.18 (Sat)		Work as previous days carried out during the day. G.O.C.op. Remainder had time in readiness to take over. Brigadier General paid a visit to locality. Fine during day, rain at night.	See P

Bn. Ridley, Major.
Commanding
29th Bn. Durham Light Infantry.

S E C R E T.   Copy No. 18

29th. Bn. DURHAM LIGHT INFANTRY.
OPERATION ORDER NO. 8.

Ref. Hazebrouck Sheet 5.a. 1/100,000 and 27, 1/40,000.

(1). The Battalion will entrain at STEENVOORDE to-morrow, 12th inst. and detrain at ST. MOMELIN.

(2). Reveille 4.0.a.m.
Breakfast 5.0.a.m.
Order of March to STEENVOORDE will be:- H.Q. Coy, 'A', 'B', 'C', and 'D' Coy.
(a). 200 yards' distance will be maintained between Companies.
(b). No smoking except during halts.
Bugle Band will parade with 'C' Coy.
Dress:-   Fighting Order (Haversack in lieu of pack). S.D. Caps.
          Steel Helmets will be carried on the left shoulder.
Haversack rations will be carried.
Head of the Column will pass Starting Point at 9.0.a.m.
Starting Point will be F.35.a.40.10.

(3). Route of march will be:- CAMP - ST. SYLVESTRE CAPPEL - WAEGEBRUGGE - WAGENBRUGE - STEENVOORDE.

(4). An Advance Party of 1 Officer and 6 Other Ranks (to include 1 N.C.O. of X.T.M.B.) will be at Church ST. SYLVESTRE CAPPEL at 9.0.a.m. to meet Lorry proceeding to St. MOMELIN.
This Party will parade at Battalion Orderly Room at 8.0.a.m.

(5). All Lewis Gun Limbers will be packed to-night and parked in Transport Lines.

(6). Blankets, Packs, surplus stores, Officers' Valises, Mess Kits, etc. will be stacked at Quartermaster's Stores by 5.30.a.m.
Blankets will be securely rolled in bundles of 10 and clearly labelled.
3 Motor Lorries will report to Quartermaster at 6.0.a.m. to convey packs, blankets and surplus ammunition to STEENVOORDE.
Quartermaster will arrange loading party from his own staff.

(7). All Tents and Shelters will be stacked by 6.30.a.m. on the road near each Companies Camp ready for loading.
O.C. 'C' Coy will detail loading party of 1. N.C.O. and 6 Other Ranks, which will be left in charge of the above Tents and Shelters.
Lorries will collect these stores (and return same to O.O. VII Corps Troops, WATTEN) after taking packs and blankets to STEENVOORDE.
The loading party will be carried on the Lorries and on completion of delivery of tents etc, will rejoin Unit at St. MOMELIN.

(8). Transport will proceed by road to St. MOMELIN Area, where it will rejoin Unit.
Head of Column will be at P.15.c.7.5. Road Junction, at 8.30.a.m.

(9). 2/Lieut. N.J. Marsh will meet Representative of Area Commandant at Battalion Orderly Room at 7.0.a.m., to hand over billets etc. He will obtain Clearing Certificate in triplicate and receipts in duplicate for all stores etc.

(10). Marching Out States will be rendered to Orderly Room by 7.0.a.m.

(11). Arrival in billets will be reported to Orderly Room immediately.

1.

(12). Falling Out Returns will be rendered to Orderly Room 1 hour after arrival in billets.

(13). ACKNOWLEDGE.

F.W.Pepper
2/Lieut & A/Adjutant.
29th. Bn. Durham Light Infantry.

11.8.18.
Issued at 9.30pm.
Copies to :-

No. 1. C.O.
No. 2. O.C. 'A' Coy.
No. 3. O.C. 'B' "
No. 4. O.C. 'C' "
No. 5. O.C. 'D' "
No. 6. 41st. I.B.
No. 7. T.O.
No. 8. Q.M.
No. 9. O.C. 'H.Q' Coy.
No.10. O.C. Signals.
No.11. Area Commandant, ST. MARIE CAPPEL.
No.12. M.O.
No.13. O.C. X.T.M.B.
No.14. O.I/c 29th.D.L.I. Bridge Guard, c/o Area Commandant, ABEELE.
No.15. C.R.E.
No.16. R.T.O. WINNIZEELE.
No.17. O.C. 62nd Field Coy. R.E.
No.18. War Diary.
No.19. File.

S E C R E T.   Copy No. 76

29th. Bn. DURHAM LIGHT INFANTRY.

OPERATION ORDER No. 9.

Ref. Hazebrouck Sheet 5.a. 1/100,000.

1. The Battalion will proceed by route march to AUDROVE to-morrow, 13th instant.

2.   Reveille 5.30.a.m.
    Breakfast 6.0.a.m.
Order of march will be :- H.Q. Coy, 'A', 'B', 'C', and 'D' Coy.
  (a). 200 yards' distance will be maintained between Companies and First Line Transport.
  (b). No smoking except during halts.
  (c). All men falling out will be given a chit by an Officer.
  (d). O.C. 'D' Coy will detail a Guard of 1 Officer and 6 Other Ranks to collect Stragglers.
Bugle Band will parade with 'D' Coy.
Dress :- Fighting Order (Haversack in lieu of pack). S.D. Caps. Steel Helmets will be carried on the left shoulder.
Head of the Column will pass Starting Point at 8.0.a.m.
Starting Point will be Cross-roads near Church, NIEURLET.

3. Route of march will be :- NIEURLET - LE BAS - SERQUES - AUDROVE.

4. An Advance Party of 2/Lieut. N.J. Marsh C.Q.M.S's and 1 N.C.O. each for Transport and H.Q. Coy will proceed on Cycles leaving Headquarters at 6.0.a.m.

5. All Lewis Gun Limbers, etc., will remain packed to-night and parked in Transport Lines.

6. Quartermaster will arrange to collect Officers' Valises and Mess Kits by 7.0.a.m.
Blankets, Packs, surplus stores, etc., will be stacked at Quartermaster's Stores by 7.0.a.m.
Lorries will report to the Area Commandant, St. MOMELIN at 9.a.m. to-morrow for the carriage of packs. Two journeys to be made if necessary.
A Guide will be detailed by this Office to report at Area Commandant's Office, WATTEN, by 8.45.a.m.
Quartermaster will arrange his own fatigue loading party.

7. Baggage and Supply Wagons will be returned to their Train Companies immediately on completion of move.

8. A Rear Party consisting of 2/Lieut. A.T. Reid and 5 men per Company will remain behind.
These men will know the billets of their Company.
A Representative of the Area Commandant will inspect billets at 8.0.a.m.
2/Lieut. A.T. Reid will obtain Clearing Certificate in triplicate.

9. Marching Out States will be rendered to Orderly Room by 7.0.a.m.

10. Arrival in billets will be reported to Orderly Room immediately.

11. Falling Out Returns will be rendered to Orderly Room 1 hour after arrival in billets.

12. ACKNOWLEDGE.

F.W.Pepper
2/Lieut & A/Adjutant.
29th. Bn. Durham Light Infantry.

12.8.18.
Issued at 9pm
Copies to

No. 1. C.O.
No. 2. O.C. 'A' Coy.
No. 3. O.C. 'B' "
No. 4. O.C. 'C' "
No. 5. O.C. 'D' "
No. 6. 41st. I.B.
No. 7. T.O.
No. 8. Q.M.
No. 9. O.C. H.Q. Coy.
No.10. O.C. Signals.
No.11. Area Commandant, St. MOMELIN.
No.12. O i/c 29th. D.L.I. Bridge Guard, c/o Area Commandant,
ABEELE.
No.13. M.O.
No.14. O i/c Stragglers.
No.15. War Diary.
No.16. File.
No.17. O.C. A.T.M.B.

SECRET.   Copy No. 18

29th. BN. DURHAM LIGHT INFANTRY.
OPERATION ORDER NO. 10.

Ref Map HAZEBROUCK S.A.
     Sheet 27.

(1) The Battalion (less Transport) will move by train from WATTEN Station to PROVEN Area to-morrow, 20th. instant, and will be accommodated in ROAD CAMP, Sheet 27, F.25.d.7.2.

(2) Head of the Column will pass the Road Junction C.3.44.54. at 7.30 a.m.
    Order of march will be :- H.Q.Coy., 'A', 'B', 'C' and 'D' Coy.
    Dress :- Battle Order. Caps S.D.
             Steel Helmet will be carried in the pack.
    Bugle Band will parade with 'A' Coy.

(3) Usual orders re march discipline will be observed.
    O.C. 'D' Coy will detail 1 Officer and 6 Other Ranks to march in rear of the Battalion to pick up stragglers.

(4) Transport which has not proceeded to-day will proceed under Cpl Heaton T. M.M. from ST.OMER Station at 8 a.m. to-morrow.
    He will arrange that Transport arrives at ST.OMER Station at 5 a.m. On completion of move, Transport will be accommodated at WILKINS CAMP, Sheet 27, F.25.a.2.9.

(5) Arrangements for Advance Party will be notified later.

(6) Entraining States will be handed in to Orderly Room by 7.0 a.m. to-morrow, showing (a) Officers, (b) Other Ranks.
    2/Lieut. F.G.W.Pepper, M.C. will be given a consolidated State and will precede the Battalion to the Station to hand State to Brigade Entraining Officer, Capt. A.W.H.Watson, M.C.

(7) 2/Lieut. G.Hattersley will report to Brigade Entraining Officer at WATTEN Station at 7.30 a.m. to-morrow to assist in the entrainment of the Brigade.

(8) Companies will arrange to be clear of billets by 7.0 a.m.
    Os.C. Companies will send Guide to Battalion Headquarters at 7 a.m. to meet Representative of Area Commandant and conduct round billets.
    O.C. 'D' Coy will detail an Officer to obtain Clearing Certificate, in triplicate, from Area Commandant's Representative.

(9) Arrival in billets will be reported to Orderly Room immediately.

(10) Falling Out Returns will be rendered to Orderly Room 1 hour after arrival in billets.

(11) 2 Lorries will report to Quartermaster at 10 p.m. to-day to convey stores, blankets, men's kits, etc. to ST.OMER Station. These Lorries will make as many journeys as required.

(12) All men's kits, Officers' Valises, blankets, stores, etc. will be stacked at Quartermaster's Stores by 10 p.m. to-day.
    Quartermaster will arrange that these are at ST.OMER Station at 5.0 a.m. to-morrow.
    He will detail 1 N.C.O. and 1 man to act as Guard over these Stores, which will remain with same until delivered at ROAD CAMP, Sheet 27, F.25.d.7.2.

(13) On arrival at PROVEN, 1 Lorry will report to convey stores from Station to ROAD CAMP.
This Lorry will make as many journeys as required.

(14) All Ranks will be warned that no N.C.O. or men is to leave the train, for any purpose whatsoever, without permission from an Officer.
N.C.O. i/c of Open Trucks will ensure that no man has his feet outside the truck.

(15) Os.C.Companies will ensure that all Sand-bags containing men's kits are clearly marked.

(16) On completion of move, Transport Officer will arrange that Baggage Wagons return to the Train Company immediately.

(17) All Water Carts and Water Bottles will be filled before entrainment and will not be filled during the journey.

(18) ACKNOWLEDGE.

[signed]
Captain & Adjutant,
20th. Bn. Durham Light Infantry.

19.8.18.
Issued at 11 a.m.
Copies to :-
No. 1. C.O.
No. 2. O.C.'A' Coy.
No. 3. O.C.'B' Coy.
No. 4. O.C.'C' Coy.
No. 5. O.C.'D' Coy.
No. 6. 41st. I.B.
No. 7. T.O.
No. 8. Q.M.
No. 9. N.C.O. i/c Transport proceeding to-morrow.
No.10. O.C.H.Q.Coy.
No.11. 2/Lieut. G.Hattersley.
No.12. 2/Lieut. F.G.W.Pepper,M.C.
No.13. O.C. Signals.
No.14. Area Commandant, WATTEN.
No.15. O i/c 20th.D.L.I.Bridge Guard, c/o Area Commandant, ABEELE.
No.16. M.O.
No.17. O i/c Stragglers.
No.18. War Diary.
No.19. File.

S E C R E T.　　　　　　　　　　　　　　　　　　　　　　　Copy No........14......

20th. Bn. DURHAM LIGHT INFANTRY.
OPERATION ORDER NO. 11.

Ref Map Sheet 28.

(1) The Battalion will relieve the 1/4th. Bn. Cheshire Regt. in the Reserve Brigade Area to-day, 27th. Instant.

(2) The Battalion will proceed by train from LUMBRES Station, J.19.c.5.7., to HOPOUTRE JUNCTION, B.27.d.6.2.
Parade 5.30 a.m.
Dress:- Battle Order.

(3) Lewis Guns, 26 Magazines per Gun, Trench Stores, etc. will be carried on the man.

(4) All surplus Lewis Gun Magazines, spare stores, Officers' Valises, Mess Kits, Men's Kits, Blankets, etc. will be stacked at Q.M. Stores by 7.30 a.m.
3 Lorries will report at Q.M. at 7.0 a.m.
These Lorries will make one journey only.
Baggage Wagons will report to Q.M. at 10.0 a.m.

(5) Transport will move by road leaving Camp at 8.30 a.m.
Route will be :- In't NOORT CAMP, L.4.b.7.2. - switch road N. of POPERINGHE - L.6.a.4.6. 28/A SH.d.3.7. - Cross roads O.3.c.3.9. - Cross roads A.23.a.4.0. to destination.
On completion of move, Transport Lines will be located at A.30.a.

(6) An Advance Party of 2/Lieut. F.O.W. Power, H.Q. 1 Officer or N.C.O. per Coy and H.Q. Coy will leave Bn. H.Q. at 5.45 a.m. on cycles to take over.
O.C. Signals will arrange cycles.
This Party will report to 151st. Infantry Brigade H.Q. by 8.0 a.m. to-day and will proceed to H.Q. 102 Infantry Brigade 28/A. 29.d.1.6. reporting there at 10.0 a.m. where guides will be provided to Bn. H.Q. of 1/4th. Bn. Cheshire Regiment.
Arrangements will be made for this party to provide Guide to meet Transport at Cross-roads A.23.a.4.0.

(7) A Rear party of 2/Lieut. H.J. March and 15 men of "B" Coy will remain and hand over the Camp to a Representative of the 1/4th. Bn. Cheshire Regt.
The above Officer will obtain Clearing Certificate in duplicate and Receipt for Army Stores.

(8) Care will be taken that all Water Bottles are filled.

(9) As Transport will not rejoin the Unit until late to-night, all necessary articles should be taken with the men on the Train. Q.M. will arrange that any missing stores to the 3 Lorry Loads allotted are taken with the Battalion on the Train.

(10) All movement East of POPERINGHE - PROVEN Road will be by Platoons and always single vehicles - 100 yards will be maintained between Platoons and between single vehicles.
No movement of transport East of VLAMERTINGHE - ELVERDINGHE Road inclusive before 8.0 p.m.

(11) On completion of relief, Battalion Headquarters will be at B.29.d.6.4.
Companies will be disposed along a general line H.8.b. and d.
Companies will take over alphabetically.

(11) a. 2 Guides per Coy and 1 for H.Q. Coy will meet Battalion at the Detraining Point.

(12) All secret maps, Defence Schemes, Aerial Photos, Schemes of work and Trench stores will be carefully taken over and lists of same forwarded to Battalion Headquarters by 6.p.m. to-day.

(13) Completion of relief will be reported to Battalion H.Q. by code phrase "ALL ROCKS RETURNED".

(14) The Battalion will move again on the 29th. instant.

(15) An Advance Party consisting of 2/Lieut. G. Hattersley, 1 Officer per Company, 1 N.C.O. per Platoon and 3 Runners from H.Q. will report at Battalion H.Q. at 4.0 p.m. and proceed to report at H.Q. 103 Infantry Brigade at 7.0 p.m. to-day.

(16) ACKNOWLEDGE.

H Cunnron
Captain & Adjutant.
20th. Bn. Durham Light Infantry.

27.8.18.
Issued at 5.45 a.m.
Copies to
No. 1. C.O.
No. 2. O.C. 'A' Coy.
No. 3. O.C. 'B' Coy.
No. 4. O.C. 'C' Coy.
No. 5. O.C. 'D' Coy.
No. 6. Adjt. I.B.
No. 7. 1/4th Bn. Cheshire Regt.
No. 8. T.O.
No. 9. Q.M.
No.10. 2/Lt. F.G.W. Pepper, M.C.
No.11. O.C. H.Q. Coy.
No.12. 2/Lt. H.J. March.
No.13. M.O.
No.14. War Diary.
No.15. File.

SECRET.   Copy No...14..

9th. Bn. DURHAM LIGHT INFANTRY.

OPERATION ORDER NO 12.

Ref Map Sheet 28 N.W.

(1) The Battalion will relieve the 8th Bn. K.O.S.B. in Brigade Reserve to-night the 28/29th August.

(2) Companies will take over Alphabetically.

(3) On completion of relief Companies will be located as follows:-
   Right   Company:- 'D' Coy. Headquarters at I.8.b.4.3.
   Forward Company:- 'C' Coy. Headquarters at I.3.b.1.3.
   Left   Company:- 'B' Coy. Headquarters at I.1.d.8.9.
   Reserve Company:- 'A' Coy. Headquarters at I.1.a.6.5.
   Battalion Headquarters will be at I.5.a.03.75.

(4) An advance party has already proceeded to the Line.

(5) Platoon Guides will meet Companies at junction of BROWN LINE and HOME FARM TRACK at H.6.a.8.9.
Companies will arrange to pass this point at 8.0 p.m. in the following order:- H.Q. Coy, 'A', 'B', 'C' and 'D' Companies.
100 yards distance will be maintained between Companies and 50 yards between Platoons.

(6) All Defence Schemes, Maps, Aeroplane photographs, work in hand, and trench stores etc. will be carefully taken over, and Lists forwarded to Battalion Headquarters by 9.0 a.m. 29th. instant.

(7) Completion of relief will be notified by following code phrase, "WATER INSUFFICIENT".

(8) Orders for handing over present area will be issued separately.

(9) Company Limbers will report to Companies at the point where they meet guides.
Battalion Headquarters' Limber will report at Headquarters at 7.0 p.m. and will go direct to ration dump.
Rations will be sent up by rail. (See Administrative Notes).

(10) All Officers' Valises and any stores to be taken to Transport Lines will be stacked at Battalion Headquarters by 6.0 p.m.
The R.S.M. will detail a guard for same.
Transport Officer will arrange to collect.

(11) Ration arrangements will be as taken over from 8th.Bn. K.O.S.B.

(12) Lieut. K. Hare and 2 runners from 'C' Coy will report to 103rd Infantry Brigade Headquarters, (H.3.b.1.4.), at 11.a.m. 28th instant for Liaison duty with Headquarters, Right Battalion, 2nd Belgian Grenadier Regt.
O.C. 'B' Coy will arrange to relieve a Liaison post at I.1.b.9.3. Strength 1 N.C.O. and 3 men. This party will report at Battalion Headquarters, 8th. K.O.S.B. at 6.p.m. 28th instant.

(13) ACKNOWLEDGE.
                                       H Ormerod
                                       Captain & Adjutant,
28.8.18.   9th. Bn. Durham Light Infantry.
Issued at 6 am
Copies to
No. 1. C.O.   Nos 7 & 8. Rear H.Q.
No. 2. O.C. 'A' Coy.   No. 9. 51st. I.B.
No. 3. O.C. 'B' Coy.   No.10. 8th.Bn. K.O.S.B.
No. 4. O.C. 'C' Coy.   No.11. War Diary.
No. 5. O.C. 'D' Coy.   No.12. File.
No. 6. O.C. H.Q. Coy.

31
Original.   Vol 4

War Diary
of
29th Battalion Durham Light Infantry
from
Sept. 1st 1918. to Sept. 30th 1918.

Volume IV.

R.W. Ridley   Lt. Col.,
29th Bn. Durham Light Infantry

Original

Army Form C. 2118.

WAR DIARY
or
INTELLIGENCE SUMMARY.

(Erase heading not required.) DURHAM LIGHT INFANTRY –
—2/9 Battn

Instructions regarding War Diaries and Intelligence Summaries are contained in F. S. Regs., Part II. and the Staff Manual respectively. Title pages will be prepared in manuscript.

Place	Date	Hour	Summary of Events and Information	Remarks and references to Appendices
YPRES	1.9.18	(Sun)	Working parties were found by the Battalion for work under the R.E. Quiet on the front.	F.Sut.O
Do.	2.9.18	(Mon)	Work on construction of new & reconstruction of old trenches &c. was carried out during the day. Brigadier General Sweeney paid a visit to the Battalion around the line. Hot dry weather. Quiet on front.	F.Sut.O
Do.	3.9.18	(Tues)	Brigadier General Sweeney D.S.O. assumed command of the 151st Infantry Brigade vice Brigadier General Kearns, 6.M.G. D.S.O. to England. Hot, fine weather. Artillery fairly active as yesterday forenoon.	F.Sut.O
Do.	4.9.18	(Wedn)	Officers from the 6th Bn. West Rgt. reported at Bn. Hd. Qrs. for inspection of dispositions &c. of this unit took under Bn.Co. carried on all during the day. Our front was by this time assuming more activity. Stillness the during day, ranged at night.	F.Sut.O
Do.	5.9.18	(Thur)	Work on trench system proceeds with Brigade reserve to the 6th Bn. Worcestr. Regt. Battalion handed over the entrances at GODERICH Station for BREAK CAMP; G.6.b (Sheet 28). Artillery Duel this day.	F.Sut.O Operation Order No.13 Appendix 15 H.
BREAK CAMP	6.9.18	(Frid)	Battalion in camp. Cleaning equipment, clothing – part bathing inspections of kits took place this day.	F.Sut.O

Sheet 28 G.6.b.

Original

Army Form C. 2118.

WAR DIARY
or
INTELLIGENCE SUMMARY
(Erase heading not required.) DURHAM. LIGHT. INFANTRY

— 29th Battn —

Instructions regarding War Diaries and Intelligence Summaries are contained in F. S. Regs., Part II. and the Staff Manual respectively. Title pages will be prepared in manuscript.

Place	Date	Hour	Summary of Events and Information	Remarks and references to Appendices
Brook Camp Sect. 28. G.6.b.	7.9.18 (Sat)		Training & instruction in various subjects carried out during the day. Specialists training done including Snipers & Scouts in the afternoon. Thunder storm during evening. Fine in afternoon & evening.	—
Do.	8.9.18 (Sun)		Divine services of all denominations were held in camp during the morning. Working party found to erect Bomb shelters at A 30 Central. R.E.s supervised. Rain all day.	—
Do.	9.9.18 (Mon)		During the day working parties were found for erecting Bomb shelters under R.E.s. At night the Battalion relieved the 33rd London Regt. R.B. in the Brown Line. Battn. Hd. Qrs. at Arrival Farm 28 N.W./B 28.d.6.4. Improvement work done on the BRIELIN line. Heavy rain.	— Operation Order No. 14 appendix No. 15
Brown Line (Arrival Farm)	10.9.18 (Tues)		Work of constructing shelters & improving trench systems carried out under R.E.s. Heavy rain.	—
Do.	11.9.18 (Wedn)		Similar duties as yesterday. In the afternoon the Commanding Officer (Major B.W.Ridley, M.C.) lectures to all officers - K.60 on "Trench Standing Orders". Fine day.	—
Do.	12.9.18 (Thurs)		Work on system carried out during the day. Raines. Operation Orders issued in connection with Batln. relieving 16th Hawkeshire Rgt. on night of 13/14th.	—

Original.

Army Form C. 2118.

WAR DIARY
or
INTELLIGENCE SUMMARY.
(Erase heading not required.) DURHAM. LIGHT. INFANTRY.
— 29th. Battn.

Instructions regarding War Diaries and Intelligence Summaries are contained in F. S. Regs., Part II. and the Staff Manual respectively. Title pages will be prepared in manuscript.

Place	Date	Hour	Summary of Events and Information	Remarks and references to Appendices
BROWN LINE & YPRES Sector.	13.9.18	Frid (Night)	The Battalion relieves the 16th Bn. Manchester Regt. in right sector, left sub-sector at night 13/14th. A & B Coys. in front line, C & D Coys. in reserve & support respectively. Battalion H.Q. in Ramparts at I.8.d.03.76. Patrols carried out. Fine weather.	4th Eliot. Operation Order No.15. Appendix No.6.
YPRES Sector	14.9.18	(Sat.)	D Coy. of this unit relieves D Coy. of the 10th Bn. Highland Light Infantry in the front line & on the right of our A & B Coys. C Coy. with up D Coy. (D.L.I.) Position in support at the ECOLE defences. B Coy. Patrols were done & a keen watch kept on "Gordon House". Fine weather.	4th Eliot. Operation Order No.16. Appendix M.
Do.	15.9.18	(Sun).	Usual duties, patrols carried out. Fine	4th Eliot.
Do.	16.9.18	(Mon)	Do. Advanced posts were established by the Battalion. Heavy rain & thunder storm.	4th Eliot.
Do.	17.9.18	(Tues)	Battn. has "Daylight patrols" in No-man's-Land. A 5.6. Rfles. taken prisoners. Excellent work was done by patrols, incompatible by patrols to get in touch with an army who were reported to have settled on their B Brigade. Fine.	4th Eliot. 4th Eliot No.1 at Night No.1 appendix to 17A.
Do.	18.9.18	(Wedn)	Usual duties &c. done during day. 1st Bn. K.O.S.B. & 7th Seaforth Highlanders sent representatives to reconnoitre our line. Fine.	4th Eliot.
Do.	19.9.18	(Thurs)	In front line. At night Battalion was relieved by 1st K.O.S.B. & 7th Seaforth Highlanders. — A, B & C Coys. by the former, D. H.Q. by the latter. Battalion entrained at GOODERICH (29/I.1.c.1.8) & detrained at WINNIZEELE, occupying billets vacated by 16th Bn. Manchesters at 27/J.23.a.2.4. (Fine weather.)	4th Eliot. Operation Order No.17. Appendix 18.

D. D. & L., London, E.C. Wt W1771/M2031 5/17 Sch. 82 Forms/C2118/14

Original.

Army Form C. 2118.

WAR DIARY
or
INTELLIGENCE SUMMARY.

(Erase heading not required.) DURHAM. LIGHT. INFANTRY — 29th Bn.

Instructions regarding War Diaries and Intelligence Summaries are contained in F.S. Regs., Part II. and the Staff Manual respectively. Title pages will be prepared in manuscript.

Place	Date	Hour	Summary of Events and Information	Remarks and references to Appendices
WINNIZEELE	20.9.18	(Fri)	Battalion was inspected for deficiencies in kit, clothes, boots &c. A Kitts parade also carried out during the day. Fine weather.	
Do.	21.9.18	(Sat)	Battalion was inspected by the Commanding Officer during morning & afternoon. Coys carried out training under own arrangements. After being inspected. A message of congratulations on the Battalion's good work in the line was sent by the General Officer Commanding the 14th Division & read out to the men by the Commanding Officer of this Battalion. Fine weather.	Appendix No "5a"
Do.	22.9.18	(Sun)	Divine Services for all denominations were held during the morning. Church of England in the Church Army Hut at WINNIZEELE. Prot: other than C. of E. in a vicinity of billets. Rains at various times.	
Do.	23.9.18	(Mon)	Battalion carried out training, including Specialists, under Company Commanders own arrangements according to programme submitted. The Commanding Officer (now Lieut. Colonel B. W. Bradley. M.C.) inspected Coys at times from 9.30 a.m - 1.30 p.m. Showery weather.	
Do.	24.9.18	(Tues)	Companies submitted programmes to Bn. H.Q. & training was done during the day in accordance. Showery in afternoon & evening. Showery in the morning.	

Original.

Army Form C. 2118.

WAR DIARY
or
INTELLIGENCE SUMMARY.

(Erase heading not required.) — 29th Battn. DURHAM LIGHT INFANTRY —

Instructions regarding War Diaries and Intelligence Summaries are contained in F. S. Regs., Part II. and the Staff Manual respectively. Title pages will be prepared in manuscript.

Place	Date	Hour	Summary of Events and Information	Remarks and references to Appendices
WINNIZEELE	25.9.18 (Wed)		During the morning parades under Coy. Commanders were carried out in accordance with programme. Corps Commander visited the Battalion – also inspected A & B. Coys. Recreational training in afternoon. Fine day.	Flwt.
Do.	26.9.18 (Thurs)		Work as yesterday was done. The Commanding Officer went to the forward area on tour of inspection. Heavy rain during the morning. Fine in afternoon clearing.	Flwt.
Do. & Reninghelst.	27.9.18 (Frid)		Battalion preparing to move from Winnizeele – Reninghelst. Entrainment took place at FUZEVILLE (28/G.34.b). Billets were occupied in detrainment at Reninghelst taken over from the 228th Field Coy Royal Engineers. Three Officers (with servants) were sent to the 14th Divisional Reception Camp at 27/L.33.c.3.5. Fine all day.	Flwt. Operation Order No. 19. Appendix No. 19.
RENINGHELST	28.9.18 (Sat)		The Battalion moved at 5 a.m. to Micmac Camp (28/G.31) in reserve to the 14th Division who were attacking South of YPRES. Remained in this Camp all day. Heavy rain throughout the day.	Flwt. Bgde Operation Orders Nos. 18, 19 & 20. Appendices Nos. 18, 19 & 20.
Micmac Camp	29.9.18 (Sun)		Attack having been successful, the Battalion moved back to billets in RENINGHELST at 4 p.m. Showery at long intervals, otherwise day fine.	Flwt.

(18604) D. D. & L., London, E.C. Wt W:7771/M2031 759,000 5/17 Sch. 52 Forms/C2118/14

Original.

Army Form C. 2118.

WAR DIARY
or
~~INTELLIGENCE SUMMARY.~~

Instructions regarding War Diaries and Intelligence Summaries are contained in F. S. Regs., Part II. and the Staff Manual respectively. Title pages will be prepared in manuscript.

— 29th Battn (Erase heading not required.) DURHAM. LIGHT. INFANTRY —

Place	Date	Hour	Summary of Events and Information	Remarks and references to Appendices
RENINGHELST	30.9.18 (Mon)		The Battalion remained in billets at this place.	New?
MESSINES			Note:— In consequence of good work done on the "Daylight Patrol at YPRES" on the 17th inst, the following H.C.C. were awarded the Military Medal (Authority Bgde R.O. No 53 of 26/9/18):— Bgde R.O. No 53 appendix No 190d	
			101857 Pte (L/Cpl) Doornbos A. A' Coy. 85612 Birch H.	
			R.W. Ridley Lieut. Col. 29/4 Bn. Durham Light Infantry.	

Original.

No 5

War Diary

of

29th Battalion Durham Light Infantry.

from

October 1st, 1918, to October 31st, 1918.

Volume V.

M. Ridley Lt. Col.,
29th Bn. Durham Light Infantry.

Original

Army Form C. 2118.

WAR DIARY
or
INTELLIGENCE SUMMARY.
(Erase heading not required.)

20th Battn. Durham Light Infantry

Instructions regarding War Diaries and Intelligence Summaries are contained in F. S. Regs., Part II. and the Staff Manual respectively. Title pages will be prepared in manuscript.

Place	Date	Hour	Summary of Events and Information	Remarks and references to Appendices
RENINGHELST	1-10-18 (Tues)		Battn moved to the Area North of MESSINES (O.33), by march north via G.38.c.1.y - LA CLYTTE - KEMMEL - WHYTSCHAETE, and relieved the 2nd Battn London Scottish in the Front Line on the night 1/2". 3 Coys in Front Line. 1 Coy in reserve. Battn HQ at GAPAARD FARM O.35.a.5.3. Weather wet	J.H. Operation Orders No. 20 & 21 Appendix No. 1.
MESSINES	2-10-18 (Wed)		Defences improved. Front actively patrolled by night. Movement by day dangerous owing to enemy observation. Hostile shelling of main roads. Weather showery	J.H.
Do.	3-10-18 (Thurs)		Improvement of defences continued, and front patrolled by night. Intermittent hostile shelling of roads. Weather showery	J.H.
Do.	4-10-18 (Fri)		"A" Coy moved forward into Front Line. Battn HQ moved to L'ESPERANCE CAB O.36.B.3.6. Artillery very active. Two sections of No. 8 Platoon "B" Coy blown up in a Dug-out, supposed cause of explosion - delayed mine. Casualties 4 killed. Weather wet	J.H.
Do.	5-10-18 (Sat)		Front patrolled by night. Work on line practically impossible owing to weather conditions, ground, & enemy observation. Weather wet. Battn was relieved on the night 5/6 by the 18th Kings Own York & Lancaster Regt. and moved into Support Area	J.H. Operation Orders No. 02-02 aa. Appendix No. 2

Original

Army Form C. 2118.

WAR DIARY
or
INTELLIGENCE SUMMARY.
(Erase heading not required.)

29th Batn. Durham Light Infantry

Instructions regarding War Diaries and Intelligence Summaries are contained in F. S. Regs., Part II. and the Staff Manual respectively. Title pages will be prepared in manuscript.

Place	Date	Hour	Summary of Events and Information	Remarks and references to Appendices
MESSINES AREA	6.10.18 (Sun)		Artillery both sides very active. Showery weather. Ground muddy	J.H.
Do.	7.10.18 (Mon)		Ground in front of support line patrolled. Vicinity of LOCK 3 (P26 & 6.5) reconnoitred with the view to establishing Batn H.Q. there. Heavy hostile shelling of vicinity L'ESPERANCE CAB 036 & 3.6. Weather showery	J.H.
Do.	8.10.18 (Tues)		Batn H.Q. moved to LOCK 3. Continued heavy hostile shelling of Battalion sector. Front actively patrolled. Weather showery	J.H.
HOUTHEM AREA	9.10.18 (Wed)		Artillery activity both sides increased, a large amount of counter battery work being done. Operation Orders issued for the relief of the 33rd Batn London Regt. (R.B.) on night 10/11th. Weather wet. Ground wet. Ground met early morning	J.H.
Do.	10.10.18 (Thurs)		Battalion relieved the 33rd Batn London Regt (R.B.) in the Front Line on the night 10/11th. 3 Coys in Front Line. 1 Coy in support. Batn. H.Q. at SCHOONVELD FARM P22 c 3.3. Weather showery. Artillery very active	Operation Order No.23 Appendix No. 3

Original.

Army Form C. 2118.

Instructions regarding War Diaries and Intelligence Summaries are contained in F. S. Regs., Part II. and the Staff Manual respectively. Title pages will be prepared in manuscript.

WAR DIARY
or
INTELLIGENCE SUMMARY.
(Erase heading not required.)

29th Battn. Durham Light Infantry

Place	Date	Hour	Summary of Events and Information	Remarks and references to Appendices
HOUTHEM AREA	11.10.18 (Fri)		Area between RIVER LYS and Front Line (P34d. P35c & d.) actively patrolled. Bridges over R. LYS reconnoitred. Artillery very active. Battn H.Q. moved to LOCK 3 (P26 t 6.5). Weather showery.	G.14
Do.	12.10.18 (Sat)		Active patrolling of front continued. Northern outskirts of COMINES and MORTE LYS reconnoitred. Many enemy M.G and T.M. posts observed. No.1 Platoon of "A" Coy was attacked at posts in vicinity of 14t. and suffered heavy casualties. Artillery very active. Weather showery. Very misty early morning.	G.14
Do.	13.10.18 (Sun)		Active patrolling as before. Efforts were made to find some of the men of the Platoon attacked yesterday (some men being known casualties) but with no success. Artillery very active. Weather showery. Ground very muddy.	G.14
COMINES AREA	14.10.18 (Mon)		R. LYS was crossed and positions taken up on S.E. side of River. New positions became untenable however during the day, and a withdrawal was made to the original positions. For Narrative of Operations on the 14th. and 15th. see Appendix No.5. Bridging Operations were carried out by the 89th Field Coy. R.E. Weather showery. Ground muddy.	G.14. Operation Order No.24 Appendix No. 4 + 5

Original

Army Form C. 2118.

Instructions regarding War Diaries and Intelligence Summaries are contained in F. S. Regs., Part II. and the Staff Manual respectively. Title pages will be prepared in manuscript.

WAR DIARY
or
INTELLIGENCE SUMMARY.
(Erase heading not required.)

29th Battn. Durham Light Infantry

Place	Date	Hour	Summary of Events and Information	Remarks and references to Appendices
COMINES AREA	14.10.18 (Mon)		Advanced Battn. H.Q. established at LA CAROTTE CAB T.29.c.05-81. Artillery very active	J.H.
"	15.10.18 (Tues)		Preceded by a Barrage which commenced at 0530, the crossing of the R. LYS was again effected with few casualties. For narrative of Operations on the 15th see Appendix No. 5. At the end of the day the following line was held. South side of COMINES approximately along the line of the RAILWAY, thence along the COMINES — WERVICQ-SUD road. Hostile artillery fairly quiet during the day. Weather fine & cold. Very misty early morning. Battalion was relieved in the front line on the night 15/16th by the 16th Battn. Manchester Regt. On relief Battn. entrained at MAI-CORNET arriving at WULVERGHEM at about 0400	J.H. Operation Order No. 24 Appendix Nos 4 & 5 Appendix No. 5
WULVERGHEM	16.10.18 (Wed)		Battn. in camp at WULVERGHEM TSa. under canvas. Ground a quagmire. Men rested and cleaned up. Weather very wet.	J.H.

Original

Army Form C.2118

WAR DIARY
or
INTELLIGENCE SUMMARY.
(Erase heading not required.)

20th Battn. Durham Light Infantry

Instructions regarding War Diaries and Intelligence Summaries are contained in F.S. Regs., Part II. and the Staff Manual respectively. Title pages will be prepared in manuscript.

Place	Date	Hour	Summary of Events and Information	Remarks and references to Appendices
WULVERGHEM	17.10.18 (Thurs)		Battalion in camp, cleaning equipment, clothing &c. Men bathed. Kits inspected, and deficiencies taken. Weather very wet. Turned very misty. Lt. Col. R.L. Ridley M.C. proceeded on leave and Major G. & Mrs. Mills assumed command.	S.F.
Do	18.10.18 (Fri)		Battalion moved at 08.10 in motor lorries to area South of COMINES. Battn. billeted in HAZEBROUCK FACTORY (V6a). Weather fine.	S.F. Aft. Fit T/Pro T/Rb S.F. Operation Order No. 26 Coomby T/No. 6 S.F. Operation Order No. 5 Coomby T/No. 5
COMINES	19.10.18 (Sat)		Battalion moved at 08.45 to march route to RONCQ Area. Men billeted in a factory close to railway. Equipments and kits cleaned and inspected. Weather fine early later wet.	S.F.
RONCQ	20.10.18 (Sun)		Battalion proceeded to the LUINGNE — HERSEAUX Area, and on arrival was billeted in LUINGNE. Inspection held. Equipments and kits cleaned. Weather fine.	S.F.
LUINGNE	21.10.18 (Mon)		Inspections held, and deficiencies made good where necessary. Weather showery.	S.F.
Do	22.10.18 (Tues)		Various inspections held, and a number of fatigue parties employed. A little training was done during the morning. Weather fine & cold	S.F.

Original

Army Form C. 2118.

WAR DIARY
or
INTELLIGENCE SUMMARY.

(Erase heading not required.) 20th Batn. Durham Light Infantry

Instructions regarding War Diaries and Intelligence Summaries are contained in F. S. Regs., Part II. and the Staff Manual respectively. Title pages will be prepared in manuscript.

Place	Date	Hour	Summary of Events and Information	Remarks and references to Appendices
LUINGNE	23/10/18 (Wed)		Training was carried out in Handling of Arms, and Squad Drill. Also Specialist subjects. The G.O.C. Major-General J. C. B. Skinner C.M.G. D.S.O. accompanied by Brig. Genl. Stoney D.S.O. inspected the boys at training during the morning.	J.H.
Do.	24/10/18 (Thurs)		Training was carried out in Close Order Drill. Outpost work, and Specialist subjects. Men bathed in the factory. A chest was held in the factory in the evening.	G.H.
Do.	25/10/18 (Fri)		Training was carried out in accordance with the programme. Reinforcements reported and were taken on the strength of the Battalion. Weather fine & cold.	J.H.
Do.	26/10/18 (Sat)		Training as yesterday. Night Operations were carried out. The exercises consisting of Outpost work, and concentration march by night. Boys engaged in sport during the afternoon. Weather fine & cold	G.H.

Original

Army Form C. 2118.

WAR DIARY
INTELLIGENCE SUMMARY.
(Erase heading not required.)

29th Batt. Durham Light Infantry

Place	Date	Hour	Summary of Events and Information	Remarks and references to Appendices
LUINGNE	27.10.18 (Sun)		The B.G.C. Brig-Genl Sweeny D.S.O. addressed all officers and senior N.C.Os at the Town Hall HERSEAUX during the morning. Divine Services were held during the day for all denominations later Survey. Weather fine early part of day – later showery.	J.H.
Do	28.10.18 (Mon)		Raining as usual in accordance with programme issued. Demonstration of Infantry work given in the afternoon. Weather fine.	J.H.
Do	29.10.18 (Tues)		Training as usual as per programme issued. A Coy. football match was held in the afternoon. Weather fine. Lt. Col R.H. Roley M.C. returned from leave and assumed command.	J.H.
Do	30.10.18 (Wed)		Coy. carried out training in accordance with the programme. One officer per Coy. and one officer of H.Q. Coy. proceeded, in the afternoon, to DOTTIGNIES to reconnoitre the Area held by the 6th Battn Wilts Regt in view of the possible relief on the following day. Weather fine Warmer.	J.H.
Do	31.10.18 (Thurs)		Limbers to packed during morning preparatory to move. Battalion moved at 1400 by march route to DOTTIGNIES relieving the 6th Battn Wilts Regt in Brigade Reserve. Weather showery.	J.H. Operation Order No 28 Appendix No. 8

R.H. Roley
Lieut. Col.
Commanding
29th Battn. Durham Light Infantry

SECRET   Appendix No. 1   No. 11

29th. BN. DURHAM LIGHT INFANTRY.
OPERATION ORDER NO. 10.

Ref Map Sheet 28.

(1) The Battalion will move to an Area North of MESSINES in O.33. to-day.

(2) Head of Column will pass Road Junction at O.35.c.1.7. at 0800, in the following order :- "D" Coy., "C", "B", "A" and H.Q.Coy., Transport.
Dress :- Battle Order.
Route will be :- O.35.c.1.7. - LA CLYTTE - KEMMEL - WHYTSCHAETE.
Movement will be by Platoons at 100 yards distance.

(3) Transport Officer will arrange for Limbers, Mess Cart, etc. to report at their respective Coy H.Q. and Battn. H.Q. by 0700.

(4) An Advance Party of 1 N.C.O. per Coy and H.Q.Coy and 1 N.C.O. from Transport Section, under 2/Lieut. A. NOTTINGHAM, will meet the Staff Captain at MESSINES Cross-roads O.32.d.5.3. at 1200.
They will have an Area allotted to them and return to meet the Battalion at the East entrance to WHYTSCHAETE Village O.15.b.3.0. at 1300.
This party will parade at Battn. H.Q. at 0730.

(5) Baggage Wagons and 3 Lorries will report at Battn. H.Q. at 0700 to convey all baggage and stores to Forward Area.
All blankets, valises, etc. will be dumped at Q.M.Stores by 0730.
Lorries may be used for more than one journey if necessary, but must not be kept later than 1800.

(6) Tents and Shelters will be drawn at O.19.b.4.0. at time to be detailed later.

(7) Rations for consumption on 2nd. instant will be delivered at the Transport Lines.
Quartermaster will send a N.C.O. to meet Supply Wagons at O.19.b.4.0. at 1500.

(8) ACKNOWLEDGE.

              Captain & Adjutant,
           29th. Bn. Durham Light Infantry.

1.10.18. 0430.
Issued at
Copies to :-
No. 1. C.O.
No. 2. O.C. "A" Coy.
No. 3. O.C. "B" Coy.
No. 4. O.C. "C" Coy.
No. 5. O.C. "D" Coy.
No. 6. O.C. H.Q.Coy.
No. 7. T.O.
No. 8. Q.M.
No. 9. 41st. Inf. Bde.
No.10. M.O.
No.11. War Diary.
No.12.   do.
No.13. File.

SECRET.   Copy No. 13

OPERATION ORDER NO. 21.

25th. Bn. DURHAM LIGHT INFANTRY.

Ref Map Sheet 28.

(1) The 25th. Bn. Durham Light Infantry will relieve the 2nd. Bn. London Scottish Regt. in the line to-night October 1st/2nd. A Battalion of 93rd. Infantry Brigade will be on the right and the 7th. Bn. Royal Irish Regt. on the left.

(2) On completion of relief, Companies will be disposed as under :-
    'B' Coy.   Right Front.
    'C' "   Centre Front.
    'D' "   Left Front.
    'A' "   Reserve.

(3) Guides for Companies will be at Battn. H.Q. at 0001. Company Commanders will report at Battn. H.Q. at that hour.

(4) The Battalion will move into the line in Battle Order. Q.M. will arrange to issue shovels, picks, bombs, etc. to Companies.

(5) Completion of relief will be reported by runner.

(6) O.C. 'D' Coy will relieve a liaison post at D.33.A.O.5.

(7) Movement in the Forward Area will be reduced to a minimum.

(8) Transport Officer will detail one limber to report to each Company at 2350 to-day.
Any surplus stores Companies may have will be sent to Q.M. Stores this evening.

(9) ACKNOWLEDGE.

                                            H Cinnerod
                                            Captain & Adjutant,
                                            25th. Bn. Durham Light Infantry.

1.10.18.
Issued at 19.45
Copies to :-

No. 1. C.O.
No. 2. O.C. 'A' Coy.
No. 3. O.C. 'B' Coy.
No. 4. O.C. 'C' Coy.
No. 5. O.C. 'D' Coy.
No. 6. O.C. H.Q. Coy.
No. 7. T.O.
No. 8. Q.M.
No. 9. 41st. Inf. Bde.
No.10. M.O.
No.11. War Diary.
No.12.   do.
No.13. File.

Appendix No. 2

S E C R E T.　　　　　　　　　　　　　　　　　　　　　　　　Copy No. 13

29th. Bn, DURHAM LIGHT INFANTRY.
OPERATION ORDER No 22.

Ref Map Sheet. 28. 1/40,000.

(1) The Battalion will be relieved in the line to-night, 5th/6th Octr. by the 18th. Bn. York & Lancaster Regt.

(2) Companies will be relieved as under :-
'B' Coy 29th D.L.I. by 'C' Coy 18th York & Lancs Regt.
'D' Coy　　"　　"　'B'　"　　　"　　　　"
'A' Coy　　"　　"　'D'　"　　　"　　　　"
'C' Coy　　"　　"　'A'　"　　　"　　　　"

(3) Guides will be provided as follows :-
'B' and 'D' Coys will arrange mutually with 'C' and 'B' Coys respectively 18th York & Lancs Regt for rendezvous and time of guides.
'A' Coy will send 5 guides to Battn.H.Q. at 8.p.m.
'C' Coy will send 5 guides to a point on the road at O.35.b.7.5. at 8.p.m.
All guides will have written instructions.

(4) After relief in the line the Battalion will take over positions as vacated by Coys of 18th York & Lancs Regt as follows:-
'A' Coy 29th D.L.I. from 'B' Coy 18th York & Lancs Regt.
'B'　"　　"　　"　'C'　"　　　"　　　　"
'C'　"　　"　　"　'A'　"　　　"　　　　"
'D'　"　　"　　"　'D'　"　　　"　　　　"
Guides will be provided by 18th York & Lancs as under :-
'B' Coy 29th. D.L.I. will arrange mutually with 'C' Coy 18th York & Lancs Regt.
'A' Coy 29th D.L.I. will arrange with 'B' Coy 18th York & Lancs Regt.
Guides for 'C', 'D' and H.Q. Coy will be at O.35.a.3.7.
Coys must send small advance parties this afternoon.

(5) All S.O.S. Signals and A.Ps. will be handed over.

(6) Rations:-　'A' and 'B' Coy will send guides for ration limbers to cross-roads in O.35.c. at 2359.
Quartermaster will arrange to deliver rations for H.Q. 'C', and 'D' Coy to new positions in O.33.a.

(7) Limbers for Lewis guns, petrol tins etc will report to 'C' and 'D' Coys ration dumps at 2300.

(8) Companies will ensure that all petrol tins are returned.

(9) Map of dispositions will be forwarded to Battn.H.Q. by 1200 Octr.6th.

(10) On completion of relief O.C. 'A' and 'B' Coys will send a runner to H.Q. 18th York & Lancs Regt who will convey any messages sent by wire to them.

(11) ACKNOWLEDGE.

　　　　　　　　　　　　　　　　　　　　　Captain & Adjutant,
　　　　　　　　　　　　　　　　　　29th. Bn. Durham Light Infantry.

5.10.18.
Issued at 133 O
Copies to :-

No. 1. C.O.
No. 2. O.C. 'A' Coy.
No. 3. O.C. 'B' Coy.
No. 4. O.C. 'C' Coy.
No. 5. O.C. 'D' Coy.
No. 6. O.C. H.Q.Coy.
No. 7. 41st. Inf. Bde.
No. 8. O.C. 18th York & Lancs Regt.
No. 9. O.C. 33rd London Regt. R.B.
No.10. O.C. 18th Durham L.I.
No. 11 & 12. Rear H.Q.
No.13. War Diary.
No.14. File.

SECRET.   29th. Bn. DURHAM LIGHT INFANTRY.   Copy No......

OPERATION ORDER No 22/A.

On relief 'C' and 'D' Coys and H.Q. Coy will not take over from 18th York & Lancs Regt but will move to areas as follows:-

'C' Coy :- to accommodation in P.26.d.
'D' Coy :- to accommodation in P.25. a & b.
H.Q. :- unknown, will be notified later.

Companies will send at once an Officer and platoon guides to reconnoitre areas.

Ration guides for 'C' and 'D' Coys should be at present Battn. H.Q. at 2300.

ACKNOWLEDGE.

Captain & Adjutant,
29th. Bn. Durham Light Infantry.

5.10.18.
Issued at
Copies to :-

O.C.'A' Coy.
O.C.'B' Coy.
O.C.'C' Coy.
O.C.'D' Coy.
41st. Inf. Bde.
T.O.
Q.M.

Appendix No. 3

SECRET.　　　　　　　　　　　　　　　　　　　　　　　　　　　Copy No......

29th. Bn. DURHAM LIGHT INFANTRY.

OPERATION ORDER. No 23.

Ref Map Sheet 28 S.W. & S.E.　1/20,000.

(1) The Battalion will relieve the 33rd. Bn. London Regt, R.B. in the Left Subsector on night 10th/11th Octr.

(2) Companies will relieve as under :-
'A' Coy 29th.D.L.I. will relieve 'A' Coy 33rd.L.R.R.B. (Right).
'B'　"　　"　　"　　"　　'C'　"　　"　　"　　" (Centre).
'C'　"　　"　　"　　"　　'D'　"　　"　　"　　" (Left).
'D'　"　　"　　"　　"　　'B'　"　　"　　"　　" (Support).

(3) 5 guides per Company for 'A', 'B', and 'C' Coys will be at P.27.d.1.2. at 1900.
5 guides for 'D' Coy and 2 for Battn.H.Q. will be at cross-roads P.21.c.9.3. at 1900.

(4) It is impossible to send advance parties but Os.C. Coys will send one Officer to-night to reconnoitre.

(5) Usual distances will be maintained.

(6) All Trench Stores, Maps, S.O.S. signals etc will be taken over and list forwarded to Battn.H.Q. by 1200 11th instant.

(7) Ration limbers with room for Lewis Guns will report to Coys at 1800.

(8) Completion of relief will be reported by code phrase "25 tins required".

(9) On relief Companies of 33rd London Regt. R.B., will take over the accommodation vacated by the Companies that relieve them in the line.
Each Company 29th. D.L.I. will detail 5 guides who will take Companies of 33rd. London Regt, R.B., from the Company H.Q. in the line back to their new area.

(10) Mens' sandbags etc for moving to Transport lines will be stacked at present ration dumps and 2 men per Company left with them. Transport Officer will arrange to collect.

(11) ACKNOWLEDGE.

　　　　　　　　　　　　　　　　　　　　H Ormerod
　　　　　　　　　　　　　　　　　　　　Captain & Adjutant.
　　　　　　　　　　　　　　　　　　　　29th. Bn. Durham Light Infantry.

9.10.18.
Issued at
Copies to

No. 1. C.O.
No. 2. O.C. 'A' Coy.　　　　　　　No. 9. 33rd London Regt, R.B.,
No. 3. O.C. 'B' Coy.　　　　　　　No.10. T.O.
No. 4. O.C. 'C' Coy.　　　　　　　No.11. .M.
No. 5. O.C. 'D' Coy.　　　　　　　No.12. M.O.
No. 6. O.C. H.Q. Coy.　　　　　　No.13. R.A. Liaison Officer.
No. 7. 41st Inf. Bde.　　　　　　　No.14. War Diary.
No. 8. 18th York & Lancs Regt.　No.15. File.

SECRET.

Appendix No. 4

Copy No. 17

29th. Bn. DURHAM LIGHT INFANTRY.

OPERATION ORDER No 24.

Refce. Sheet 28 – 1/40,000.

(1) The 2nd Army in conjunction with the French and Belgian Forces is to resume the offensive at H hour on J Day. The time and date will be notified later.

(2) The 30th Division of the Xth Corps on left of 14th Division will attack the hostile position on the front CRUCIFIX FARM, P.30.b. to KLIJTHOLEN, Q.8.c.

(3) The objective of the attack is the approximate line :-

Railway in P.30.c & b - Q.25.a. - RESKE Village (incl) - Road junction Q.17.d.1.2.

The 30th Division will exploit success by pushing out patrols to occupy and hold WARVICQ and the line of the LYS, P.36, Q 31, Q 26.

(4) The attack will be covered by an Artillery barrage which will commence at H – 2 minutes.
One Brigade R.F.A., 14th D.A. and one Coy., 14th Bn., M.G.Corps, will co-operate with 30th Division.

(5) In case the pressure of the Xth Corps attack induces the enemy to relinquish his positions on the Divisional front the following preparations will be made.

(a) Battalions in the line of 41st Inf. Bde. will push patrols across the River LYS, supporting them by stronger bodies and eventually to continue the advance.
(b) The direction of the advance, if made, will be across the River LYS, and then Eastward towards the line of the high ground in W.2 & W.8. If misty patrols must proceed by compass bearing set at due East.
(c) The 43rd Inf. Bde. will be in a position west of MESSINES in Support, and will be prepared to follow up the advance.
(d) Footbridges will be thrown across the River LYS for Infantry at the following points :-
V.3.a.2.0.
V.9.b.5.9.
P.35.d.0.3.
P.36.a.2.7.
and a bridge at V.2.b.5.9. to carry Field Guns.

1.

(6) It is possible that the enemy may attempt to hold COMINES and will not withdraw for some time. The closest touch is to be kept with the enemy, day and night, and energetic patrols and scouts' must be pushed forward across the River LYS. as soon as pn
The best chance of crossing will probably be by the bridge at P.36.a.2.7.
Mutual support by means of Lewis Gun covering fire must be given by all Companies on every possible occasion to Patrols attempting to cross the River.

(7) Advanced Battn. H.Q. will be established at H hour at 'A' Coy H.Q. (P.27.d.7.5.).
Advanced Brigade H.Qrs. will be at ESPERANCE CABT. (O.35.b.3.8.)

(8) Companies immediately on receipt of J Day will form a dump of all mens' greatcoats, and spare stores.
The proposed location of these dumps will be forwarded to H.Q. at once.
Transport Officer will arrange to collect.
A small guard should be left by each Company.

(9) Companies should ensure that they are complete with Battle Stores. These can be made up from Coy dumps. Companies will wire for any stores they require.

(10) ACKNOWLEDGE.

H. Ormerod
Captain & Adjutant.
29th. Bn. Durham Light Infantry.

13.10.18.
Issued at
Copies to :-

No. 1. C.O.
No. 2. O.C. 'A' Coy.
No. 3. O.C. 'B' Coy.
No. 4. O.C. 'C' Coy.
No. 5. O.C. 'D' Coy.
No. 6. T.O.
No. 7. Q.M.
No. 8. 2nd i/c.
No. 9. I.O.
No.10. M.O.
No.11. R.S.M.
No.12. War Diary.
No.13. File.

S E C R E T.

To:-

All Coys, 29th Durham L.I.
2.C.
T.O.
M.O.
I.O.
R.S.M.
O.C. 14th.Bn. M.G. Corps.
O.C. 41st L.T.M.Bty.
Hqrs. 41st Inf. Bde.
O.C. 89th Coy. R.E.

} for information

(1) In continuation of Operation Order No 24, the Objective allotted to the 14th Division has been modified.
Should the situation to-night or to-morrow morning admit the 30th Division will push forward advanced guards to occupy PAUL BUC, and ROUSBACQUE.
The 14th Division will be prepared on receipt of orders from Corps to push forward strong patrols across the river and if successful, to establish a Bridgehead covering COMINES and connecting with 30th Division on the tributary of the LYS which runs through W 7 and W 1.

(2) The 41st Inf. Bde will be prepared to carry out the above operation, and will advance with 2 battalions in the line.
The 29th D.L.I will be on the left, and the 33rd London Regt., R.B. on the right.
The 18th York & Lancs Regt will be in reserve in P.32.c.

(3) The objective allotted to the 41st Inf. Bde will be from the River LYS in V.8.d along the railway line from STAYS ROAD past STROM House (V.10.c), to contour 20 in V.11.b, thence to contour 20 in W.1.c.

(4) The Right boundary of the 41st Inf. Bde will be from V.c.d.5.0, thence due East along the grid line
The Left boundary will be approximately the line of the BEC DE IR BOIS.
The Inter-battalion boundary will be from V.4.b.2.0 to V.5.c.0.0 thence due East along the grid line.

(5) The Operation will be carried out by strong patrols pushing forward at zero to the LYS in advance of bridging detachments of 89th Field Coy, R.E.
Bridges will be thrown across the LYS at points detailed in Operation Order No 24.
Further details as to the co-operation with the R.E. detachments will be given verbally to Os. C. Coys.

(6) The advance will be covered by an Artillery barrage lasting from zero to zero plus 40, and by M.G. and T.M. fire wherever possible.

(7) The dispositions for the attack at zero will be as follows:-

Right Coy, 'A' Coy.   3 Platoons situated as at present.
Coy H.Q. at P.34.a.5.0

Centre Coy, 'B' Coy.   3 Platoons in Front line in their present situation.
1 Platoon and Coy.H.Q. at P.35.a.0.5.

Left Coy, 'C' Coy.   2 Platoons in Front line in present situation.
2 Platoons and Coy H.Q. in and around School building at P.29.d.4.0

Reserve Coy, 'D' Coy.   4 Platoons in shell holes and dugouts in P.28 c and d.
Coy H.Q. at P.28.c.65.50

Battn.H.Q.   At LA CAROTTE CAST. (P.29.c.0.9)

Os.C Coys will make all necessary arrangements to have their Companies in position by zero - 1 hour.

(8) Details as to the method of advance will be issued in writing to all recipients of this order.

(9) O.C. 'C' Coy will detail 1 Officer to report to O.C. Battn on left for keeping liaison during the advance.

(10) Zero hour will be notified later.

(11) ACKNOWLEDGE.

H Ennew
Captain & Adjutant,
29th. Bn. Durham Light Infantry.

14.10.18.

SECRET.

Appendix No. 5.

Headquarters,
    41st. Infantry Brigade.

I beg to report as follows on the operations from 13th. to 16th. October.

On taking over the Brigade Left Sector on 10th October, I was warned that a retirement of the enemy from the COMINES - WARNETON Sector was imminent. I therefore kept my front actively patrolled night and day, in order to keep touch. Patrolling by day was most difficult, the slightest movement by my men along the roads drew heavy Machine Gun fire from the enemy. Although I could not get close to the enemy by day, the constant alertness shown by the enemy and the heavy Machine Gun fire gave me the information I required.

On the evening of 13th. instant I received orders to be prepared to cooperate in the advance by the Xth Corps immediately North of my Sector. My instructions were to keep close touch with the enemy and to push out patrols if signs of an enemy withdrawal were observed.

At 05.35 of the 14th. instant, the attack by the 30th. Division on my left started.

I received early information that their objectives had been gained and that a withdrawal by the enemy was imminent. At the same time I was ordered to push forward patrols to keep touch.

I immediately sent forward small reconnaissance patrols from my three forward Companies along the Railway down to the River at the North East corner of the town and to the bend in the road 800 yards North East of this point. At these two points arrangements had been made to throw bridges across the river in cooperation with a detachment of 89th. Field Coy. R.E. These bridges were known as Bridge 3 and Bridge 4 respectively.

My Patrols went out at 10.30 and both reached the river bank unmolested. They walked openly along the river bank, and thoroughly inspected the original bridges, which they found destroyed, without a shot being fired or any notice taken.

This result and also the fact that the hostile shelling and Machine Gun fire, very active on the previous day, had been practically nil throughout the morning, led me to suspect that the enemy had withdrawn from the town. I therefore decided to push patrols across the river to verify this. To enable this to be done, I had to call on the R.E. to throw the bridges across, as no means of crossing at that time existed. I also asked the O.C. 41st. T.M.B. to cut wire in the opposite banks to make a lane through for my men. At 13.00., after ½ hour's bombardment by Trench Mortars, strong patrols, covered by scouts, advanced simultaneously towards Bridges 3 and 4. Two Companies were held in readiness to follow across in case the attempt was successful. At Bridge 4 the ground is perfectly open and the operations had to be carried out in full view of the enemy. A Lewis Gun Section proceeded ahead at this point and took up a position on the North bank close to the bridge. The R.E. immediately followed and commenced to lay a duckboard footbridge 2ft.6" wide across the river. This was roughly laid across and the Lewis Gun Section were sent across to the South side to cover the R.E. while the latter completed the Bridge. At the same time the gun of the 14th. Machine Gun Bn. was mounted in a house on the COMINES - WARNETON Road, 600 yards North West of the Bridge. So far not a shot had been fired, but as soon as the Lewis Gun Section was in position on the South side, hostile Machine Gun fire was opened from HOOGMOOTH FARM, HAZEBROUCK FACTORY, THE DISTILLERY and from a point approximately 2,000 yards due South of Bridge 3. Two more Sections were sent across, however, without loss and a second

Platoon sent forward in readiness to follow up.

The enemy now opened heavy Artillery fire which was concentrated on the bridge and road in the vicinity of GODSHUIS. From 14.00 to 17.00 this area was very heavily shelled unceasingly. The task however was not yet abandoned and my Lewis guns replied actively on the enemy. Meanwhile the Patrol which proceeded to Bridge 3 had also reached the river and a bridge had been commenced. This was carried out unmolested until fire had been opened on the Bridge 4 party. As soon as this occurred fire was also opened on Bridge 3 from M.Gs. on the South bank 50 yards distant, the DISTILLERY, and the Island between MORTE LYS and the LYS. Heavy shelling commenced here too at the same time.

The op Preparation at this point was most difficult: the original bridge had been more damaged than Bridge 4 and my Patrol could not get across in advance of the R.E. detachment. Two Lewis Gun teams took up a position therefore on the Railway Embankment on the North side and opened heavy fire on the opposite bank. Casualties began to occur very rapidly both amongst the R.E. detachment and my own men. Lieut Halliwell, 89th. Field Coy, R.E. did very gallant work in supervising the erection of the Bridge. He managed to crawl across and although very badly wounded lay still on the South bank under cover controlling the operations. 2/Lieut. C.A. Carter of my Battalion also displayed very gallant conduct here in leading his platoon. He stood up openly on the Embankment, and fired with a Lewis Gun from his shoulder at the Machine guns on the opposite bank until he was killed.

Until 15.30 the resistance shown was so great and the casualties heavy that I decided to withdraw all my men from Bridge 3 which was not quite completed, and to stop any more men from crossing over Bridge 4.

I had definately ascertained that the enemy positions were still strongly held, and had definately located 3 new Machine gun posts which were afterwards dealt with by our own Artillery.

I determined however to try and hold the Bridgehead at Bridge 3 if I could.

One Lewis gun section was therefore left on the South side, and the remainder of the men withdrawn to the shelter of the Buildings on the road behind.

At 19.00 the shelling at this point was so very great that I began to fear that the Bridge would be destroyed and the Lewis gun section cut off. At the same time, this section was being badly enfladed by the enemy Machine gun at HOOGNOUTH FARM. I then decided to withdraw my men entirely to their original positions. This was accomplished without loss.

Lieut. NAim, 89th Field Coy, R.E. rendered very valuable work in the construction of this Bridge which was kept constantly maintained in spite of the severe shelling. No further attempt to cross was made that evening. A further patrol was sent out at 17.00 to the Island between MORTE LYS and the LYS. They succeeded in crossing but heavy resistance from Machine Guns was encountered. The Officer in charge, 2/Lieut. A. Dean. M.C. was very badly wounded, (since died), and a Sergeant and 1 man killed. The patrol remained out there however and was withdrawn after dark to enable the Island to be bombarded by our Artillery. This patrol performed useful work in drawing Machine gun fire off the party in Bridge 3 who were in great difficulties.

The shelling and Machine gun fire was kept up incessantly over the whole area KORENTJIE - FIVE WAYS - and the BAS-WARNETON Road - COMINES ROAD throughout the night until 3 a.m. when the Machine gun fire entirely ceased, and the shelling became considerably less.

At 1.a.m. on 15th I received orders that the advance of the 41st. Brigade across the river which had been arranged in the event of an enemy withdrawal would be carried out at 05.30 on the morning of 15th instant. I held a hurried conference with Company Commanders and issued verbally for the advance. The situation was a little difficult. I had to expect strong resistance at the ISLAND, when moreover a crossing of the main river was impossible, owing to the Bridge having been destroyed, and also at Bridge 3 where I had had such serious losses the previous afternoon.

I decided therefore that I should have to be prepared to send my whole Battalion across Bridge 4 where I felt fairly confident I should be successful when assisted by the Artillery barrage and co-operation from Battalions on my left and right.

I arranged therefore for my Reserve Company and my Left Company, less 2 Platoons which were very exhausted after the previous afternoons' attempt, to cross and advance behind the barrage to a line running from Bridge 3 to the bend in the river 750 yards South East of Bridge 4, in two lines. One Platoon of my centre Company was sent to Bridge 3 to attempt to cross and join up on the South side with the other 2 Companies on my left. The remainding 3 Platoons with the 2 exhausted Platoons of my Left Company I kept back in the COMINES - WERVICQ Road in Battalion Reserve until I saw how the situated developed. One platoon of my Right Company was ordered to advance along the Main Road into the Town across MORTE LYS and clear out the Machine Gun posts in the House here, the 2 remaining Platoons of this Company being ready to follow them up in Support. I was under difficulty too in having only 1 R.E. Officer and 2 Sappers left to assist me in Bridging, but Bridge 4 was still intact, and I risked the chance of it being presently destroyed and sent the R.E. Party to devote all their attention to Bridge 3 which had not been quite completely.

At 05.300 the barrage opened, and my men started to cross the River, no retaliation or opposition was met with, and by 06.15 my 2 Forward Companies had reached the objective I had given them, and had pushed out Patrols in front. Bridge 3 had been completed and 1 Platoon had crossed and joined up on their Left as ordered. It soon became clear that the town and ground in front had been evacuated. My line was advanced to the general line BRidge 3 - HAZEBROUCK FACTORY - Junction of the BEC DES BOIS with the River LYS. I then sent forward the 2 Platoons of my Left Company, which had been kept in Reserve, across Bridge 4 to take up a position on the South side of the River in Support of my Front Line. The 3 Reserve Platoons of my Centre Company, and the whole of my Right Company, less 1 Platoon employed to carry up Reserve S.A.A., were sent across Bridge 3 to mop up the Town.

This was methodically carried out. No opposition was met with, and no signs of the enemy discovered. By 11.00 the Town was completely cleared and a line established on the South side of the Town approximately along the line of the Railway, thence along the COMINES - WERVICQ-SUD Road. I now decised not to make any further advance for the present for the following reasons :-

Firstly, my men were very tired after a very trying 18 days in the Line.

Secondly, the situation on both my flanks was very obscure.

I had received information that Bridge 2 on the West side of the Town had not been crossed by the 33rd, London Regt. R.B., and had the 30th Division on my Left, for no apparent reason, made no attempt to advance from the line of the BAS WARNETON-WERVICQ Road.

I therefore moved my 4 Companies into Line, with Platoons distributed in depth, also split up into small section posts which were immediately defensible.

Patrols were sent out to WERVICQ SUD and ROSSIGNY FARM.

I also sent back a message requesting that the 30th Divn might be asked to move forward to the Line of the LYS in line with me.   This after some delay was eventually done, and Liaison was obtained with them at The HOSPITAL 1000 yards South West of WERVICQ.

Subsequently my right flank was advanced 500 yards and Liaison established with the 53rd. London Regt, R.B.

This position was held until taken over by 15th. Bn. Manchester Regt on the night 15th/16th October.

B.W. Ridley   Lieut-Colonel,
              Commanding,
        29th. Bn. Durham Light Infantry.

17.10.18.

Appendix No. 6

SECRET.   Copy No. 12

29th. Bn. DURHAM LIGHT INFANTRY.
OPERATION ORDER No. 26.

Refce. Map Sheet 28 S.E.

(1) The Battalion will move to-day, 13th instant by march route to the ROMCQ Area.

(2) Order of march will be H.Q. "B", "C", "D", and "E" Coys. Head of the column will be at "B" Coys Mess at 07.45 hours.
    Dress:-   Battle order.   Caps S.D.
    200 yards distance between Companies will be maintained.

(3) Route will be NEWTON-NUS – HOUSEHOLT – OUBA CROSS (V.G.c.3.4.) – ROMCQ.

(4) All Officers' Valises, blankets, men's beddings, shovels etc will be dumped near the main road at 0700 hours. Transport Officer will collect.

(5) Lewis Gun limbers will report to Companies at once.

(6) Lewis Gun limbers, Field kitchens and Water carts will move with the Battalion.
    Transport other than above will proceed to ROMCQ by following route :- CORNET'S – NEWTON NUS – HOUSEHOLT – OUBA CROSS (V.G.c.3.4.) – ROMCQ, to pass the point cross roads P.25.a.85.7.5 at 0800. hours.

(7) No extra Transport will be available for Q.M. Stores.

(8) An Advance party consisting of 2/Lieut. P.G.W. Pepper. M.C. 1 N.C.O per Coy and 1 each for Transport and H.Q. Coy will leave Battn.H.Q. at 0700 and report to Staff Capt at X.5.c.05.40 at 08.15 hours.

(9) ACKNOWLEDGE.

[signature]
Captain & Adjutant.
13.10.18.   29th. Bn. Durham Light Infantry.
Issued at 0400.
Copies to :-

No. 1. C.O.   No. 7. 2/Lieut. P.G.W. Pepper. M.C.
No. 2. O.C. "A" Coy.   No. 8. Q.M.
No. 3. O.C. "B" Coy.   No. 9. T.O.
No. 4. O.C. "C" Coy.   No.10. M.O.
No. 5. O.C. "D" Coy.   No.11. War Diary.
No. 6. O.C. H.Q. Coy.   No.12. File.

S E C R E T.   Copy No...........

Appendix No. 4

29th. Bn. DURHAM LIGHT INFANTRY.

OPERATION ORDER No 27.

Refce. Map Sheets 28 29 & 37.

(1) The Battalion will continue the march to-day and proceed to the LUINGNE - HARSEAUX Area.

(2) Order of march will be :- H.Q. Coy. 'A', 'B', 'C', and 'D' Coys. Transport.
Head of the Column will be at 28/X.14.a.8.1. to 09.30 hours.
Dress:-   Battle Order. Caps. S.D.
300 yards distance between Companies will be maintained.
Usual distances will be maintained between vehicles.

(3) Route will be Cross roads 28/X.27.b.7.7 - Cross roads 28/S.25.b.5.4.- thence through MUSCRON to LUINGNE.

(4) All Officers' Valises, blankets, men's sandbags, shovels etc will be dumped at entrance to FACTORY near Battn.H.Q. at 08.00 hours.

(5) 2 Lorries are allotted for conveyance of kit, blankets etc for ONE journey only, and under no consideration will these Lorries be delayed.
Q.M. will arrange for guides to be at RONCQ CHURCH at 14.00 to collect Lorries.

(6) Rations will be delivered to Transport Lines on completion of march.
Billeting Officer will be notified at the place at which guides will be required.

(7) Attention is directed to the various orders which have been issued with regard to march discipline.   These orders must be strictly enforced.

(8) Lewis Gun limbers will report to Companies at 07.00 hours.

(9) An Advance Party consisting of Lieut. G. Hattersley, 1 N.C.O per Coy, and 1 each for Transport and H.Q. Coy will leave Battn.H.Q. at 07.30 and report to A/Staff Capt at the Church at LUINGNE (29/S.23.d.5.7) at 10.00.
Guides will meet Battalion at LUINGNE CHURCH.

(10) Certificate will be rendered to Battn.H.Q. by 08.30 that Billets are in a clean condition.

(11) Acknowledge.

G.W.Pepper.
2/Lieut. & A/Adjutant.
20.10.18.   29th. Bn. Durham Light Infantry.

20.10.18.
Issued at 01.30.
Copies to :-

No. 1. M.O.
No. 2. O.C. 'A' Coy.
No. 3. O.C. 'B' Coy.
No. 4. O.C. 'C' Coy.
No. 5. O.C. 'D' Coy.
No. 6. O.C. H.Q. Coy.

No. 7. Lieut. G. Hattersley.
No. 8. T.O.
No. 9. Q.M.
No.10. M.O.
No.11. War Diary.
No.12. File.

SECRET.   *Appendix No. 8*   Copy No. 13

29th. Bn. DURHAM LIGHT INFANTRY.

OPERATION ORDER No 28

Refce Maps Sheet 29 & 37 1/40,000.

(1) The Battalion will relieve the 6th.Bn. Wilts Regt, in Brigade Reserve ~~kxxxxxxx~~ to-day.

(2) (a) Order of march will be :- H.Q.Coy, 'A', 'B', 'C', and 'D' Coys.
  (b) Head of the column to pass point 29/S.23.d.6.7. at 14.00
  (c) 200 yards distance will be maintained between Platoons.
  (d) Dress :- Battle Order (Jerkin in Pack) Caps S.D.
  (e) Route :- PETIT VOISINAGE - OROMBIOM - DOTTIGNIES.
  (f) O.C. 'C' Coy will detail Stragglers Party of 1 Officer and 6 Other Ranks.
  Falling Out Returns will be rendered to Orderly Room immediately on arrival in new area.

(3) An Advance Party of :-
  1 Officer per Company,
  1 Officer from H.Q. Company.
  5 Other Ranks per Company.
  2 Other Ranks from H.Q. Coy.
  1 Other Rank from Transport.
  will parade at the Church LUINGNE, at 09.30 and proceed to Headquarters, 6th.Bn. Wilts Regt at 37/B.5.a.3.7. Senior Officer to take charge of the party.

(4) The Advance party will provide guides to meet the battalion at the entrance to DOTTIGNIES.

(5) O.C. 'A' Coy will detail a rear party of 1 Officer and 15 Other Ranks who will obtain Clearing Certificate from Area Commandant.
  Each Company and H.Q. Coy will detail a man who knows his Company billets to report to the above Officer at Battn. Headquarters at 14.00.

(6) All aeroplane photographs, trench maps, trench stores etc, will be carefully taken over. Complete List of any stores etc taken over to reach Battn.H.Q. by 20.00 to-day.

(7) All Officers' kits, blankets, sandbags, surplus stores etc, of 'A', 'B', 'C', and H.Q. Companies will be stacked at at Q.M. Stores by 12.30.
  Those of 'D' Coy will be stacked near Church at same time. Q.M. will collect.

(8) O.C. Coys and H.Q. Coy, Transport Officer and Q.M. will obtain "Certificat de bien vivre", from all billetees, and forward to Orderly Room.
  Billets will be ready for inspection by 14.00.

(9) Arrival in billets and location of Company H.Q. will be reported to Battn.H.Q. immediately.

(10) ACKNOWLEDGE.

H Cromwell
Captain & Adjutant.
29th. Bn. Durham Light Infantry.

31.10.18.

31.10.18.
Issued at 0800
Copies to :-

No. 1. C.O.
No. 2. O.C. 'A' Coy.
No. 3. O.C. 'B' Coy.
No. 4. O.C. 'C' Coy.
No. 5. O.C. 'D' Coy.
No. 6. O.C. H.Q. Coy.
No. 7. 41st I.Bde.
No. 8. T.O.
No. 9. Q.M.
No.10. M.O.
No.11. 2/Lieut. R.V. Atkins.
No.12. 6th. Bn. Wilts Regt.
No.13 & 14. War Diary.
No.15. File.

War Diary

SECRET.   Copy No. 11

29th. Bn. DURHAM LIGHT INFANTRY.

OPERATION ORDER. No. 15.   (Appendix No. 4)

Ref Map Sheet 28.

(1) The Battalion will be relieved in the Reserve Line by the 6th.
    Bn. Wiltshire Regiment, (less 1 Company), on night 5th/6th
    September.

(2) Companies will be relieved alphabetically.
    'A' Company will be relieved by 1 Platoon, and 'B' Company
    by 3 Platoons.

(3) On completion of relief the Battalion will entrain at
    GOODERICH (I.1.c.2.5.), and detrain at G.6.a.7.5.
    The Battalion will be accommodated in BRAKE CAMP.

(4) An advance party from 6th. Bn. Wiltshire Regt of 1 Officer
    and 5 Other Ranks per Company will arrive at SALVATION CORNER
    at 8.p.m. 4th September.
    Headquarters and Companies will detail guides to meet them.
    Quartermaster will arrange to take over BRAKE CAMP from 6th.
    Bn. Wilts Regt, on afternoon of 5th September.

(5) All Trench Stores, Defence Schemes, Maps, Aeroplane photographs,
    A. A. Posts, work in hand etc, will be carefully handed over.
    Lists to Battalion Headquarters by 12 noon 5th September.

(6) Working parties will be handed over by Battalion Headquarters,
    but Companies will point out the location of work.

(7) 4 Guides for Battalion Headquarters, 1 per Company Headquarters,
    and 1 per Platoon, will report to 2/Lieut. F.O.W. Pepper M.C.
    at GOODERICH STATION at 9.15.p.m. 5th September.
    They will have written instructions. These guides should
    reconnoitre the route by daylight.
    Route by cross-roads I.7.b.6.5.

(8) Liaison Officers and runners will be relieved during the day.
    Liaison posts will be relieved by 7.p.m.
    O.C. 'B' Coy will send guide to SALVATION CORNER at 8.0.p.m.

(9) Company stores will be taken with the men on the train.
    Any that cannot be so carried will be dumped at the Station
    and a guard left.
    Transport Officer will detail one limber to collect these stores.
    O.C. 'A' Coy will send the Transport Officer a guide to-night,
    who knows the location of the Station.

1.

(10) Quartermaster will arrange for guides to meet Companies at the detraining point.

(11) Transport Officer will arrange for two limbers to be at the detraining point to carry Stores to Camp.

(12) Completion of relief will be reported by code phrase:-
"R.E. Ingent, OOO Saratoga".

(13) ACKNOWLEDGE.

H Ormerod
Captain & Adjutant.
29th. Bn. Durham Light Infantry.

4.9.18.
Issued at 5.15pm
Copies to:-
No. 1. C.O.
No. 2. O.C. 'A' Coy.
No. 3. O.C. 'B' Coy.
No. 4. O.C. 'C' Coy.
No. 5. O.C. 'D' Coy.
No. 6. O.C. H.Q. Coy.
No. 7. 2/Lieut. F.C.W. Pepper. M.O.
No. 8. 41st. I.Bde.
No. 9. Q.M.
No.10. T.O.
No.11. War Diary.
No.12. File.
No.13. 6th Bn Wilts Regt.

SECRET.   Copy No. 14

29th. Bn. DURHAM LIGHT INFANTRY.
OPERATION ORDER NO.14.

Appendix No. 15

Ref Map 28 N.W.

(1) The Battalion will relieve the 33rd. London Regt., R.B. in the BROWN LINE on night September 9/10th.

(2) Companies will relieve alphabetically.
On completion of relief, Company H.Q. will be as follows:-
   'A' Company   H.4.b.6.8.
   'B'   "   H.5.d.7.9.
   'C'   "   H.5.c.5.1.
   'D'   "   H.5.b.20.45.
   Battn H.Q.   ARRIVAL FARM. (B.28.d.6.4.).

(3) An Advance Party per Company of 1 Officer, 1 N.C.O. and 4 Platoon Runners, and 1 Officer, 2 N.C.O's and 2 Runners for Headquarters will report to Headquarters, 33rd. Bn. London Regt., R.B. at 3.0.p.m. to-morrow.
The Runners of the above party will act as Guides for the Battalion at rendezvous to be fixed by Company Commander.

(4) Route will be by 'A' Track.
Order of march:- 'B' Coy, 'C', 'D', 'A', - H.Q. Coy.
Usual distances will be maintained.
'B' Company will leave Camp at 7.30.p.m.
Companies will reconnoitre 'A' Track to-morrow morning.

(5) All Maps, Stores and work in hand will be carefully taken over.
Lists to be at Battn H.Q. by 9.0.a.m. on 10th instant.

(6) A Map of Dispositions will be forwarded to H.Q. by 4.0.p.m. on 10th instant.

(7) Completion of relief will be reported to Battn H.Q.

(8) Company Limbers will report to Companies at 6.45.p.m. for transport of Lewis Guns, Mess Boxes and other Company Stores.
All Officers' Valises, men's sandbags and other Stores for BROWN LINE will be stacked at H.Q. by 5.0.p.m.
Quartermaster will arrange to deliver to new H.Q.
Blankets and other Stores to be taken to Rear H.Q. will be stacked at same place and time but on separate dump.
Quartermaster will collect.

(9) Rations will be delivered to new Company H.Q. to-morrow.

(10) Quartermaster will arrange to hand over BRAKE CAMP to an Officer of 33rd. Bn. London Regt. R.B., to-morrow afternoon.
Receipted Lists of Area Stores and Clearing Certificate (in duplicate) will be handed in by him to H.Q.

(11) O.C. 'B' Coy will detail 1 senior N.C.O. and 15 men as Rear Party. They will report to Quartermaster at a time to be notified by him, and will not leave until he has obtained Clearing Certificate.

1.

(12) Working Parties for 9th. and 10th. instant will be found as under:-

    9th instant.   'B' Coy.
                         2 Sections to report to R.E. Corporal at the cross-roads A.30.central at 9.0.a.m.
                         They will work under the orders of the Divisional Bombing Officer.
                         Haversack Rations will be taken.

    10th instant.   'C' Coy.
                         2 Platoons will meet Guides from 61st. Field Coy. R.E. at 28/H.6.a.3.6. at 7.0.a.m.
                         They will work on BRIFLIN Line under orders of C.R.E.
                         Shovels only will be taken.
                         1 Platoon to meet Guides from 61st. Field Coy. R.E. at 28/H.5.b.3.8. at 7.0.a.m. for work on BRIFLIN Line under orders of C.R.E.
                         Shovels only will be taken.

(13) ACKNOWLEDGE.

                                                     Captain & Adjutant.
                                      29th. Bn. Durham Light Infantry.

8.9.18.
Issued at 7.45pm
Copies to :-

No. 1. C.O.
No. 2. O.C. 'A' Coy.
No. 3. O.C. 'B' Coy.
No. 4. O.C. 'C' Coy.
No. 5. O.C. 'D' Coy.
No. 6. O.C. H.Q. Coy.
No. 7. 41st. I.B.
No. 8. T.O.
No. 9. Q.M.
No.10. 33rd L.Rgt. R.B.,
No.11. Area Commandant.
No.12. War Diary.
No.13. File.

S E C R E T.　　　　　　　　　　　　　　　　　　　　　　　　Copy No. 12.

29th. Bn. DURHAM LIGHT INFANTRY.

OPERATION ORDER No 16.　　　Apendix No 16

(1) The Battalion will relieve the 16th Bn. Manchester Regt, in the right sector, left sub-sector, on night 13/14th September. 18th Bn. York & Lancs Regt will be on the left and 43rd Infantry Brigade on the right.

(2) Companies will relieve as under :-
'A' Coy 29th D.L.I. relieve 'D' Coy 16th Manchester Regt.
'B'　"　　"　　"　　"　'A'　"　　"　　"
'C'　"　　"　　"　　"　'B'　"　　"　　"
'D'　"　　"　　"　　"　'C'　"　　"　　"

(3) On completion of relief companies will be disposed as under :-
'A' Company .. Right Front. Headquarters. I 15 b 7.7.
'B'　　"　　.. Left Front.　　　"　　　　I 9 d 2.7.
'D'　　"　　.. Support.　　　　"　　　　ECOLE
'C'　　"　　.. Reserve.　　　　"　　　　I 8 d 6.4.
Battalion Headquarters at I 8 d 05.76.

(4) An advance party as already detailed will proceed to the line to-night.

(5) Platoon Guides will meet Companies at SALVATION CORNER at 8.p.m. Companies will arrange to pass this point in following order :- A Coy, 'B', 'D', 'C', and H.Q. Coy. Usual distances will be maintained.

(6) All work in hand, trench stores etc, will be carefully taken over and lists forwarded to Battn H.Q.

(7) One Officer (to be detailed later) and 2 runners of 'C' Coy, will report to Headquarters, 42nd Infantry Brigade at 10.a.m. 13th instant, for Liaison duty with Right Battalion, Belgian Grenadier Regiment.

(8) R.S.M. will detail one bugler to report to each Company by 6.p.m. 13th inst. Companies will detail one runner to report to Headquarters for temporary duty at the same time.

(9) Completion of relief will be reported in B.A.B. code.

(10) Lewis Gun limbers will report to Companies at their respective ration dumps at 7.15.p.m. These limbers will have the rations in them.

(11) All stores to be taken to Wagon Lines will be stacked by
    8 p.m. at following dumps. One man per Company will be left
    in charge.
    'A' Company and Headquarters at ARRIVAL FARM.
    'B', 'C', and 'D' Companies at H 5 b 0.5.
    Transport Officer will collect.

(12) ACKNOWLEDGE.

                                              Captain & Adjutant,
                              29th. Bn. Durham Light Infantry.

12.9.18.
Issued at 10.30 p.m.
Copies to:-
No. 1. C.O.
No. 2. O.C. 'A' Coy.
No. 3. O.C. 'B' Coy.
No. 4. O.C. 'C' Coy.
No. 5. O.C. 'D' Coy.
No. 6. O.C. H.Q. Coy.
No. 7. 41st. I.B.
No. 8. T.O.
No. 9. Q.M.
No.10. M.O.
No.11. 16th Manchester Regt.
No.12. War Diary.
No.13. File.

SECRET.   29th. Bn. DURHAM LIGHT INFANTRY.   Copy No. 12
                               OPERATION ORDER No 16.   Appendix No. 17

Ref Map Sheet 28 N.W.

(1) (a) 'D' Company, 29th. Bn. Durham Light Infantry will relieve
        'D' Company, 18th. Bn. Highland Light Infantry in the Line
        to-night 14/15th instant.
    (b) 'B' Company 23rd London Regt. (R.B.) will relieve 'C'
        Company 29th. D.L.I. in the YPRES DEFENCES.
    (c) 'C' Coy 29th D.L.I. will occupy positions in the ECOLE
        DEFENCES vacated by 'D' Company, 29th D.L.I.

(2) On completion of relief 'D' Coy will be Right Forward Company
    with its Headquarters at I.15 b 1.2.
    'A' Coy will be Centre Company.
    'B' "   "   " Left   "
    'C' "   "   " Reserve with Headquarters in the ECOLE.

(3) O.C. Companies will arrange guides themselves.
    The Company of 23rd London Regt. R.B., will commence to move
    about 6.p.m.
    'D' Coy will move at 6.45.p.m.

(4) All stores, defence schemes etc will be taken over and lists
    forwarded to Battn H.Q.

(5) Rations for 'D' Coy will be unloaded at LILLE GATE. 'D' Coy
    will arrange to push forward from there. Highland Light Infantry
    are arranging to hand over full water tins.
    These will be refilled at the ECOLE next night.
    'C' Coy will arrange to fill all water tins for the Battalion
    from to-night.
    Companies will now push forward their own rations and water
    from the ECOLE Dump.

(6) Companies will wire code word "BOMBS" when they commence to move.

(7) Completion of relief will be reported by B.A.B.

(8) ACKNOWLEDGE.
                                            J H Ormerod
                                            Captain & Adjutant.
14.9.B.   29th. Bn. Durham Light Infantry.
Issued at 12.30/p.m.
Copies to:-
No. 1. C.O.   No. 4. O.C. 'C' Coy.   No. 8. 31st I.B.
No. 2. O.C. 'A' Coy.   No. 5. O.C. 'D' Coy.   No. 9. 18th. H.L.I.
No. 3. O.C. 'B' Coy.   No. 6. M.O.   No.10. 23rd.Lond Regt. R.B.,
                       No. 7. Q.M.   No.11. 18th Y & Lancs Regt.
                                               No.12. I.O.
                                               No.13. War Diary.
                                               No.14. File.

S E C R E T. 20th. Bn. DURHAM LIGHT INFANTRY.   Copy No......

OPERATION ORDER No. 17.   Appendix No 18

Ref Map Sheet 27/28.

(1) The Battalion will be relieved to-night 19/20th September as
under:-
'D' Coy. 20th. D.L.I.   by 'B' Coy. 1st. K.O.S.B.
'A' "   "   "   "   'C' "   "   "
'C' "   "   "   "   'A' "   "   "
'B' "   "   "   "   'B' "   7th. Seaforths.
Battn. H.Q. by H.Q. 7th Seaforths.

(2) An advance party has already reported to Companies.

(3) Time and rendezvous for guides will be notified later.
One guide per platoon.
One per Company H.Q. and 2 for Battn H.Q. will be provided.
All guides will have written instructions.
2/Lieut. A. Nottingham will be in charge of guides of 'A', 'C',
and 'D' Companies.
'B' Coy will send a Senior N.C.O. with theirs.

(4) Companies will hand over S.O.S. Bugle Posts.

(5) All trench stores, maps, defence schemes, work in hand etc will
be handed over and receipts obtained.
A list of trench stores will be forwarded to Orderly Room by
7.p.m. to-day.

(6) Battle dumps, (circulated under R.69), will be handed over by
Companies in whose sector they are.

(7) Completion of relief will be reported in B.A.B. Code.

(8) On relief Battalion will entrain at GOODRICH 28/I 1 c 1.5, and
detrain at WIMM ELM.
Battalion will occupy billets vacated by 16th. Bn. Manchester
Regt at 27/J 23 a 2.4.

(9) Transport Officer will detail 2 limbers to report to Battn H.Q.
for conveyance of stores.
All company stores and Lewis Guns will be carried by the men on
the train.

(10) Quartermaster will arrange for guides to meet Battalion at
detraining point.

(11) Rear Headquarters are moving under orders received direct from
Brigade Headquarters.

1.

S E C R E T.

(12) All Companies will arrange that petrol tins are at the
     refilling point and will arrange to hand them over there.

(13) ACKNOWLEDGE.

                                   H. Amcurd
                                Captain & Adjutant.
                            20th. Bn. Durham Light Infantry.

19.9.18.
Issued at
Copies to :-
No. 1. C.O.
No. 2. O.C. 'A' Coy.
No. 3. O.C. 'B' Coy.
No. 4. O.C. 'C' Coy.
No. 5. O.C. 'D' Coy.
No. 6. O.C. H.Q. Coy.
No. 7. 41st. I.B.
No. 8. Rear H.Q.
No. 9. M.O.
No.10. 1st. K.O.S.B.
No.11. 7th Seaforths.
No.12. War Diary.
No.13. File.

B.L.O.H.L.I.   Copy No. 13

24th Bn. HIGHLAND LIGHT INFANTRY.

OPERATION ORDER No. 19.   Appendix No. 19

(1) The Battalion will move to-day, by train, to the PETERSFIELD Area.
Transport will move at time and under instructions issued for for move on 25th instant.

(2) The Battalion will entrain at PETERSFIELD JUNCTION at 6.0 p.m. and detrain at SHEXVILLE, 10/R.B.R.b.
Companies will arrange to arrive at Station in the following order:- "A" Coy, "B", "C", H.Q. and "D" Coy, first company to arrive at 5.45 p.m.
Dress:- Battle Order.

(3) O.C. "B" and "D" Coys will each detail 1 Officer to supervise entraining, to report at PETERSFIELD Station at 5.30 p.m.
On completion of move Batt.H.Q. will be at 28/G.5.a.n.8.4. and Companies billeted in the "SHEXVILLE" Area.
Billets will be taken over from 208th Field Company, R.E.

(4) An Advance Party as under will proceed to Brigade Headquarters, PETERSFIELD, at 12 noon to-day.
Parade Batt.H.Q. 10.30 a.m.
  2/Lieut. J. Evans.
  1 N.C.O. per Company.
  2 N.C.O's from H.Q. Company.
1 N.C.O. will proceed to 14th Divisional Reception Camp to take over accommodation for Details.

(5) 3 lorries will report to Brigade H.Q. at 2 p.m. to-day
Lorries will do 1 journey only.
Quartermaster will send 1 guide to report at Brigade H.Q. at 1.45 p.m. to act as guide for these lorries.

(6) Lieut. H.A. Mitchell, 2/Lieut. H. de Caux, and 2/Lieut. F.O.F. Foster, R.C. (with servants) will rendezvous at Brigade H.Q. at 2.00 p.m. to-day, to proceed to 14th Divisional Reception Camp at 27/A.35.c.0.30, and not as before stated.

(6A) Quartermaster will arrange for the kits of these Officers to be dumped at the Reception Camp.

(7) Supplies for consumption 25th instant, will be delivered by lorry to Quartermaster's Stores.
Refilling Point on September 25th and onwards will be at 28/G.71.c.6.0. on PETERSFIELD - SHEXVILLE Road.

(8) 1 Limber will report to each Company at 4.30 a.m. to convey Lewis Guns and magazines to the Station.

(9) All stores, surplus kits etc, will be collected by Quartermaster at 11 noon to-day, and conveyed to PETERSFIELD Arch.

1.

(10) Companies will render Certificate to Battn.H.Q. by 4.p.m. to-day, that billets have been left in a clean and sanitary condition.

(11) Arrival in billets of any men will be reported to Battn. H.Q. immediately.

(12) ACKNOWLEDGE.

                                 Captain & Adjutant,
                       20th. Bn. Durham Light Infantry.

27.5.16.
Issued at 3.30 a.m.
Copies to :-
No. 1. C.O.
No. 2. O.C. 'A' Coy.
No. 3. O.C. 'B' Coy.
No. 4. O.C. 'C' Coy.
No. 5. O.C. 'D' Coy.
No. 6. O.C. H.Q. Coy.
No. 7. Qrm. M.S.
No. 8. T.O.
No. 9. M.O.
No.10. T.O.
No.11. Area Commandant, WINCHESTER.
No.12. War Diary.
No.13.   do
No.14. File.

Original.

WD 6

War Diary

of

29th Battalion The Durham Light Infantry

from

November 1st, 1918, to November 30th, 1918.

Volume VI.

B.W. Ridley, Lt. Col.,
Comg. 29th Bn. Durham Light Infantry.

Original

Army Form C. 2118.

WAR DIARY
or
INTELLIGENCE SUMMARY.
(Erase heading not required.)

29th Batt. Durham Light Infantry

Place	Date	Hour	Summary of Events and Information	Remarks and references to Appendices
DOTTIGNIES	1/11/18 (Fri)		Companies carried out training for Two hours during the morning in accordance with the programme. The C.O. and 2nd in Command, also several officers visited the front line during the afternoon to reconnoitre the position held by the 33rd London Regt. (R.B.). Weather fine. Hostile shelling of E. outskirt of DOTTIGNIES	G.H.
Do.	2/11/18 (Sat)		Training as yesterday carried out. Several officers reconnoitred front line. Weather showery. Hostile artillery shelled the village during the night (2/3rd), and a billet of "D" Coy was hit (3 killed 3 wounded).	G.H.
Do.	3/11/18 (Sun)		During the night 3rd/4th Hostile artillery again shelled DOTTIGNIES causing damage to buildings. Adjutant of the Battn. shelled by night. The new line billeted in Toelline. Weather fine.	G.H.
Do.	4/11/18 (Mon)		Training was carried out as per programme for Two hours during the morning. One officer per Coy. reconnoitred the position held by the 33rd L.R. (R.B.), in view of the relief the following day. Weather very fine. Hostile artillery active	G.H.

Original

Army Form C. 2118.

WAR DIARY
or
INTELLIGENCE SUMMARY.
(Erase heading not required.)

29th Battn. Durham Light Infantry

Place	Date	Hour	Summary of Events and Information	Remarks and references to Appendices
DOTTIGNIES	5-11-18 (Tues)		Battalion relieved the 33rd Battn. London Regt. (R.B.) on the night 5/6 in the Left Battn. Sector. "B" Coy. in the Front line. "A""C"&"D" Coys in Close Support. (HELCHIN SECTOR) Heavy hostile shelling intermittently throughout night 5/6. Weather very wet.	T.H. Operation Order No. 29. Appendix No. 1
ST. GENOIS AREA	6-11-18 (Wed)		Coys improved and repaired posts and billets where necessary. Hostile concentration shelling. The line was re-adjusted on the night 6/7. "D" Coy. D.L.I. (Left Support) took over that part of the line held by "B" Coy. 18th Battn. Yorks and Lancs. H.Q. and one platoon of "D" Coy. 19 L.I. relieved H.Q. and two platoons of "A" Coy. 19 L.I. were on relief, accommodated at GAVRE FARM. Weather very wet.	T.H. Operation Order No. 30 Appendix No. 2
do.	7-11-18 (Thurs)		Intermittent heavy hostile shelling. Enemy heavily bombarded all squares in battalion area from 15-30 to 19-00. "D" Coy. (Left front Coy) were relieved on the night 7/8 by the 4th Battn. Worcester Regt. and on relief moved into positions vacated by "D" Coy. yesterday. Weather showery. Bridges Nos. 1,2,&3 if ground shewn to little reconnoitred. Bridges were found to be practically impassable owing to shell fire and the wind rising.	T.H. Operation Order No. 31 Appendix No. 3

Signal

Army Form C. 2118.

WAR DIARY
or
INTELLIGENCE SUMMARY.
(Erase heading not required.)

29th Batn. Durham Light Infantry

Place	Date	Hour	Summary of Events and Information	Remarks and references to Appendices
ST. GENOIS AREA.	8-11-18 (Fri)		Hostile shelling and M.G. fire very much decreased. Battalion was relieved on the night 8/9th by the 10th Batn. Highland Infantry. On relief the Battalion proceeded by march route to HERSEAUX, and were accommodated in billets. Weather showery.	Junction Order No. 32. Appendix No. 4. J.H.
HERSEAUX	9-11-18 (Sat)		Battalion in kilts cleaning up. Inspections held and deficiencies taken. Weather very fine.	J.H.
Do.	10-11-18 (Sun)		Church of England service was held during the morning in a field adjoining the Transport Lines. At C.of E. Football match were held in the afternoon. Weather fine.	J.H.
Do.	11-11-18 (Mon)		A message was received early morning stating that an Armistice had been officially signed (message from Brigade H.Q). The Coys. carried out two hours training during the morning, and one hours recreational training in the afternoon. Deficiencies were made up so far as possible. Weather fine & dull. A further message was received from	J.H.

Original

Army Form C. 2118.

WAR DIARY
or
INTELLIGENCE SUMMARY.
(Erase heading not required.)

29th Batt. Durham Light Infantry

Instructions regarding War Diaries and Intelligence Summaries are contained in F. S. Regs., Part II. and the Staff Manual respectively. Title pages will be prepared in manuscript.

Place	Date	Hour	Summary of Events and Information	Remarks and references to Appendices
HERSEAUX	11.11.18 (Mon)		Brigade H.Q. during the day to the effect that hostilities cease at 11.00 today.	
do.	12.11.18 (Tues)		Our Turn's training in the morning, and one Turn's nocturnal training was carried out in accordance with the programme submitted by Coys. Weather very fine. cold	G.K.
do.	13.11.18 (Wed)		Training was carried out as yesterday. A football match was held in the afternoon H.Q. Coy. D.L.I. v. "C" Coy. L.R. (R.B.). Preparation was made and Operation Orders issued for the move to the BONDUES Area.	G.K.
do.	14.11.18 (Thurs)		Battalion moved at 0945 by march route to the BONDUES Area, and was accommodated in billets on arrival. The majority of the billets were houses evacuated by the civilian population. Battn. H.Q. at VERT BOIS CHATEAU. Weather fine fresh.	G.K. Operation Order No.33 Operation Order No.5.

Original

Army Form C. 2118.

WAR DIARY
or
INTELLIGENCE SUMMARY.
(Erase heading not required.)

29th Batt. Durham Light Infantry

Place	Date	Hour	Summary of Events and Information	Remarks and references to Appendices
BONDUES AREA	15.11.18 (Fri.)		Coys carried out Training in Company and Platoon Drill, and were also instructed in the correct fitting of Equipment. One hour's recreational training was carried out in the afternoon. Weather fine & cold.	G.H.
do	16.11.18 (Sat.)		Training was carried out in Battalion, Company & Platoon Drill, and Handling of Arms. The C.O. inspected Companies in the morning. A Rugby Football Match was played in the afternoon. 29th D.L.I. v. 13th K.R.R. (R.B). Resulted in heather line. All Battle Stores were handed in.	G.H.
do	17.11.18 (Sun.)		Divine Services were held during the morning for all Denominations. 3 Officers and 32 men attended a Voluntary Service of Thanksgiving at the "Cirque" TURCOING, commencing at 15.30. A Football match was held in the afternoon Officers v. Sergeants. Weather fine day cold.	G.H.

Original

Army Form C. 2118.

Instructions regarding War Diaries and Intelligence
Summaries are contained in F. S. Regs., Part II.
and the Staff Manual respectively. Title pages
will be prepared in manuscript.

WAR DIARY
INTELLIGENCE SUMMARY.
(Erase heading not required.)

29th Bn. Durham Light Infantry

Place	Date	Hour	Summary of Events and Information	Remarks and references to Appendices
BONDUES AREA	18.11.18 (Mon)		General Inspection held in the morning by Brig-Genl. Twenty B.S.O. Battalion carried out a few movements in the Ceremonial Drill. Recreational training in the afternoon. Weather fine, very cold.	G.K.
do.	19.11.18 (Tue)		A rehearsal of the inspection of the 41st Infy. Bde. by the Corps Commander was carried out on A & B Coys training ground. A football match was played in the afternoon. H.Q. v D. Coy. Weather fine. Heather frost.	G.K.
do.	20.11.18 (Wed)		Training was carried out in accordance with programme submitted by Coys. 53 Reinforcements arrived and were taken on the strength of the Battalion. 4 O/rs & 360 O.R. attended a lecture given by Lt. Commdr. Pierre-Simon R.S.O. R.N. at the Cinema Palace, Grande Rue, ROUBAIX at 14.30. Subject :- "Work of the British Navy during the War." A football match was held in the afternoon "C" Coy. v "B" Coy. Weather fine. cold. Very foggy.	G.K.

Original

Army Form C. 2118.

WAR DIARY
or
INTELLIGENCE SUMMARY.
(Erase heading not required.) 20th Batt. Durham Light Infantry

Place	Date	Hour	Summary of Events and Information	Remarks and references to Appendices
BONDUES AREA	20/11/18 (Wed)		Coy training was carried out in Ceremonial Drill. A great improvement was noticed in the smartness & fitting of equipment. Recreational training as usual. Weather fine.	G.H.
do.	22/11/18 (Fri)		Battalion carried out Training in Ceremonial Drill. Bath Parade attended a lecture in the afternoon by the B.G.C. 41st. Inft. Bgde on a native in the Colonies. Weather fine.	G.H.
			BONDUES School Hall. Subject "England & the Colonies". Weather fine.	G.H.
do.	23/11/18 (Sat)		The Commanding Officer inspected the mens kits equipment and billets during the morning. Recreational training in the afternoon as usual. Weather fine.	G.H.
do.	24/11/18 (Sun)		Divine Service was held during the morning for all denominations. The final in the Company Football Competition was played in the afternoon. H.Q. v. C. Coy. Weather fine.	G.H.
do.	25/11/18 (Mon)		Coys. carried out Arms Drill in the morning and one hours Recreational Training in the afternoon. Men bathed during the day. Weather fine. One officer, a reinforcement, reported Duros Today on the strength of the Battalion.	G.H.

Original

Army Form C. 2118.

WAR DIARY
or
INTELLIGENCE SUMMARY

(Erase heading not required.)

29th Battn. Durham Light Infantry

Place	Date	Hour	Summary of Events and Information	Remarks and references to Appendices
BONDUES AREA	24/11/18 (Sun)		A rehearsal of the Brigade Ceremonial Parade was held in the morning. A Boxing Competition was held in the afternoon on the grounds of the Chateau Kent Bois. One Officer re-inforcement reported and was taken on the strength of the Battalion. Weather fine	G.H.
do	25/11/18 (Mon)		A General Inspection of the 151st Inf. Bgde. was held in the morning by Lieut. Genl. Sir Beauvoir de Lisle K.C.B. D.S.O. commanding XV Corps. A Football Match was played between 29th D.L.I. & 33rd & R. (R.B.) & St Heather line. Four officers re-inforcements reported and were taken on the strength of the Battalion.	G.H.
do	26/11/18 (Tues)		Training as per programme submitted. A cross country run was held in the morning. Recreational Training in the afternoon. Battalion Officers Mess was commenced at Chateau Kent Bois. Four officers re-inforcements reported & were taken on the strength of the Battalion. Weather wet.	G.H.

Original

Army Form C. 2118.

WAR DIARY
or
INTELLIGENCE SUMMARY
(Erase heading not required) 29th Batt. Durham Light Infantry

Place	Date	Hour	Summary of Events and Information	Remarks and references to Appendices
BONDUES AREA	29/11/18 (Fri)		Battalion Drill carried out. Brig. Genl. Twenty D.S.O. inspected the new billets. A Batty of 93 Offrs. and O.R. attended a lecture given by Major D. Pollen. Dinner at the "CIRQUE" Cinema Hotel Grande Place TURCOING at 14.30. Subject "Demobilisation and Reconstruction." Recreational Training as usual in the afternoon. Weather fine.	S.H.
do.	30/11/18 (Sat)		C.O. inspected billets. Kits & equipment in the morning after which a meeting was held to discuss educational questions, all officers and Instructors being present. It was decided to commence classes at once. M.O. inspected Companies, Football match in the afternoon Stables v. Pioneers. Weather fine & cold	S.H.

P.W. Ridley Lieut. Col.
Commanding
29th Battn. Durham Light Infantry

Appendix No. 1.

O R D E R S.   20th. Bn. DURHAM LIGHT INFANTRY.   Copy No. 6.

TRENCHES SHEET 20 & 29.

Refer Maps Sheet 20 & 37.

(1) The Battalion will relieve 22nd. London Regt, R.B., in the Left Battalion Sector to-night 5th/6th November.

(2) Companies will relieve alphabetically.
    On completion of relief Companies will be disposed as under:—

    'B' Coy.   Front Line
    'A' "   Close Support.
    'C' "   Right   "
    'D' "   Left   "

(3) Head of the column will be at 37/D.2.c.5.0. at 18.30 hrs.
    Order of march will be 'B','A','C','D' & HQ.
    100 yards distance between Platoons will be maintained.

(4) An Advance party of 1 Officer, and 1 N.C.O. per Coy will report to Major, 22nd London Regt, R.B., at 15.00 hours.

(5) 5 Guides per Company will be at P

(6) All A.Fs. Trench stores etc, will be taken over, and lists forwarded to Battn.H.Q. by 09.00 hrs on 6th Nov.

(7) Completion of relief to be notified to Battn.H.Q. immediately.

(8) Lewis gun limbers and 2 limbers for H.Q. will report at 12.45 hours.

(9) All blankets, Officers' valises etc, will be stacked in Coy dumps by 16.00 hrs, and guard detailed in charge. D.M. will collect.

(10) "Certificate de bon Vivre" will be obtained in respect of each billet vacated.

(11) Present Billets will be taken over by 22nd London Regt, R.B.

(12) O.s.C. Coys and H.Q. Coy will each detail a man who knows his Coy billets to report to Battn.H.Q. at 15.00 to meet representative of the Area Commdt and conduct round billets.

(13) ACKNOWLEDGE.
                                                H Cameron
                                                Capt. & Adjutant,
                                                20th. Bn. Durham Light Infantry.
5.11.18.
Issued at:-
Copies to:-
No. 1. C.O.   No. 9. C.M.
No. 2. O.C. 'A' Coy.   No.10. M.O.
No. 3. O.C. 'B' Coy.   No.11. Area Commdt, DOMICHIES.
No. 4. O.C. 'C' Coy.   No.12. 22nd London Regt, R.B.
No. 5. O.C. 'D' Coy.   No.13. B/Batt. R.V. Adam.
No. 6. O.C. H.Q. Coy.   No.14. War Diary.
No. 7. Capt. Tpt O.   No.15.   do
No. 8. I.O.   No.16. File

D. H. Cox.

Appendix No. 2

SECRET　　　　　　　　　　　　　　　　　　　　Copy No. ......

29th. Bn. DURHAM LIGHT INFANTRY.

OPERATION ORDER No. 30.

Refce:- Map Sheets 28 & 37.

(1) Following re-adjustments of the Line will take place to-night.

   (a) 'D' Coy, 29th D.L.I. will relieve 'B' Coy 18th York & Lancs Regt in the line from U.30.c. central to C.4.a.9.2.
   This includes the two right posts of 'B' Coy, 29th D.L.I.
   H.Q. and one platoon of 'D' Coy will relieve H.Q. and 2 platoons of 'A' Coy, in BELGIUM Village.
   Guides from 18th York & Lancs Regt will be at Chateau at 37/C.4.a.6.6. at 17.00.
   O.C. 'D' Coy will arrange for guides from 'B' and 'A' Coys.

   (b) The H.Q. and 2 Platoons of 'A' Coy on relief will be accommodated in GAVRE FARM.
   O.C. 'A' Coy will reconnoitre accommodation.

(2) Completion of relief to be reported to Battn. H.Q.

(3) List of Trench stores taken over will be forwarded to H.Q. as soon as possible.

(4) 'A' and 'D' Coys will forward a disposition map of new positions.

　　　　　　　　　　　　　　　　H. Emmerson
　　　　　　　　　　　　　　　　Capt. & Adjutant,
　　　　　　　　　　　　　　　　29th. Bn. Durham Light Infantry.

6.11.18.
Issued at :
Copies to :-

No. 1. C.O.
No. 2. O.C. 'A' Coy.
No. 3. O.C. 'B' Coy.
No. 4. O.C. 'C' Coy.
No. 5. O.C. 'D' Coy.
No. 6. 41st Inf. Bde.
No. 7. 18th Y. & L. Regt.
No. 8. T.O.
No. 9. War Diary.
No.10.　do
No.11. File.

Appendix No 3

SECRET.   Copy No. 10

29th. Bn. DURHAM LIGHT INFANTRY.

OPERATION ORDER No 31.

Refce. Map Sheet 29 1/40,000.

(1) 'B' Coy, 29th. D.L.I. will be relieved to-night Octr 6th/7th, by a unit of the 88th Inf Bde (either 4th Worcester Regt or 2nd Hampshire Regt.).

(2) O.C. 'B' Coy will detail intelligent guides under an Officer on the scale of one for Coy H.Q. and one per platoon to be at road-junction U.11.a.1.6. at 16.15 hrs. The officer in charge will be in possession of information as to number of posts to be handed over, numbers holding exact post and whether post is rifle or L.G.

(3) On completion of relief 'B' Coy will move into positions vacated by 'D' Coy yesterday.
O.C. 'B' Coy should arrange to reconnoitre.

(4) Completion of relief and arrival in new positions to be reported in B.A.B. code.

(5) A list of Trench stores handed over will be forwarded to Battn. H.Q. as soon as possible.

(6) All Companies will send ration guides to H.Q. at 17.30 hrs.

(7) ACKNOWLEDGE.

                                        [signature]
                                        Capt. & Adjutant,
                                        29th. Bn. Durham Light Infantry.

7.11.18.
Issued as
Copies to :-
No. 1. C.O.
No. 2. O.C. 'A' Coy.   No. 14. File.
No. 3. O.C. 'B' Coy.
No. 4. O.C. 'C' Coy.
No. 5. O.C. 'D' Coy.
No. 6. Left Battn.
No. 7. Rear H.Q.
No. 8. 41st Inf Bde.
No. 9. M.O.
No.10. Art. Liaison Offr.
No.11. I.O.
No.12 & 13. War Diary.

Appendix No. 4

SECRET.   Copy No. 6

22nd. Bn. DURHAM LIGHT INFANTRY.

OPERATION ORDER No 32.

Refce. Maps 29 & 37.

(1) The Battalion will be relieved in the line by 10th. Bn. Highland Infantry on night 8/9th.

(2) Companies will be relieved as under :-
   'A' Coy, 22th D.L.I. by 'A' Coy, 10th. H.L.I.
   'B'   "   by 'B'   "
   'C'   "   by 'D'   "
   'D'   "   by 'C'   "

(3) Guides on the following scale :-
   1 per Coy H.Q.
   1 per Platoon.
   2 from Battn. H.Q.
   to rendezvous at :-
   'C' Coy at 29/U.21.c.7.7.   (at
   H.Q. 'A', 'B', & 'D' Coys on Railway at U.21.b.9.4.(17.30

(4) All A.Pr. Trench Stores, etc., to be handed over and Lists forwarded to Battn. H.Q. by 08.00 9th inst.

(5) Completion of relief to be reported by code phrase "WATER NOT REQUIRED".

(6) On relief, Companies and Trench Mortar Officer will form a dump of Lewis Guns, drums, stores, etc. at their present ration dumps.
A man who knows this dump will be sent to Battn. H.Q. at 19.30 hrs.
Transport Officer will detail one limber per Company, one for Trench Mortars and two for Battn. H.Q. to be at Battn. H.Q. at 20.00 hrs.
Riders at Eastern entrance to DOTTIGNIES. at 23.00 hrs.

(7) On relief, Battalion will take over billets vacated by a Unit of 42nd. Infantry Brigade.
Headquarters will be at 37/A.5.d.2.2.
Transport Lines at 37/A.5.b.2.2.
All movement will be by Platoons at 200 yards distance.

(8) Quartermaster will arrange to take over new billets and arrange to meet Battalion on arrival.

(9) No extra transport will be allowed for moving Rear H.Q. Transport can commence moving stores to new location after 11.00 hrs.

(10) Arrival in billets to be reported immediately.

(11) ACKNOWLEDGE.

H Cinnamon
Captain & Adjutant.
29th. Bn. Durham Light Infantry.

8.11.18.
Issued at 0400.
Copies to :-

No. 1. C.O.
No. 2. O.C. 'A' Coy.
No. 3. O.C. 'B' Coy.
No. 4. O.C. 'C' Coy.
No. 5. O.C. 'D' Coy.
No. 6. O.C. H.Q. Coy.
No. 7. T.O.
No. 8. Q.M.
No. 9. 41st Inf. Bde.
No. 10. 18th K. & C.
No. 11. 4th. Worcestershire Regt.
No. 12. 2/Lt. R.V. Atkins.
No. 13. M.O.
No. 14. O.C. Signals.
No. 15. File.
No. 16. (War
No. 17. (Diary.

Appendix No.5

SECRET.   Copy No. 6

29th. Bn. DURHAM LIGHT INFANTRY.

OPERATION ORDER No. 83.

Ref: Map 36 - 37 1/40,000.

(1) The Battalion will move by route march to-morrow, November 14th to the BUISSES Area.
    Headquarters will be at 36/F.13.a.2.9.

(2) Head of the column will be at 37/A.5.d.0.5. at 08.45 hrs.
    Order of march will be H.Q. Coy, 'A', 'B', 'C', and 'D' Coys, Transport.
    Route will be :- WATTRELOS - TOURCOING - LINSELLES - X roads 36/F.7.d.52.75.
    100 yards distance will be maintained between Companies, and Transport.
    Twenty five yards to be maintained between each group of six wagons.
    Dress:- Full marching order (less Haversack and Greatcoat), Cape. S.D. jackets in pack, steel helmets outside the pack.

(3) O.C. 'D' Coy will detail an Officer and 6 Other Ranks to act as Stragglers Party.

(4) O.C. 'C' Coy will detail party of 1 Officer and 1 Platoon to act as Rear party. Each company will send one man to report to this Officer, who knows the Company billets.
    This Officer will obtain Clearing Certificate from Area Commandant.
    Each company will obtain "certificat de bien vivre" for each billet.

(5) An Advance party of Lieut.C.Hattersley, 1 N.C.O. per coy, H.Q. and Transport, will rendezvous at Headquarters at 08.00 hrs, and proceed on cycles to meet Staff Capt. at 36/F.13.a.9.7. at 09.15 hours.

(6) All Officers' Valises, blankets etc., will be stacked at Q.M. Stores by 07.00 hrs.
    2 lorries will be at Brigade H.Q. at 07.00 hrs.
    Q.M. will send guides.

(7) Arrival in billets and falling out certificates will be notified to Battn. H.Q. immediately.

(8) ACKNOWLEDGE.
                                                     H.Cameron
                                                 Captain & Adjutant,
                                          29th. Bn. Durham Light Infantry.
    The Commanding Officer desires that strict attention be paid to march discipline.

13.11.18.
Issued at 22.45 hrs.
Copies to :-

No. 1. C.O.   No. 8. M.O.
No. 2. O.C. 'A' Coy.   No. 9. T.O.
No. 3. O.C. 'B' Coy.   No. 10. Q.M.
No. 4. O.C. 'C' Coy.   No. 11. 2/Lieut. R.V. Atkins.
No. 5. O.C. 'D' Coy.   No. 12. Area Commdt, HERSEAUX.
No. 6. O.C. H.Q. Coy.   No. 13. War Diary.
No. 7. 41st Inf. Bde.   No. 14.   do
                                     No. 15. File.

Original.

War Diary
of
29th Battalion the Durham Light Infantry.
from
December 1st 1918 to December 31st 1918.

Volume VII.

G. Whitehead, Major,
29th Bn. Durham Light Infantry.

Original

Army Form C. 2118.

WAR DIARY
INTELLIGENCE SUMMARY

(Erase heading not required.)

29th Battn. Durham Light Infantry

Instructions regarding War Diaries and Intelligence Summaries are contained in F. S. Regs., Part II. and the Staff Manual respectively. Title pages will be prepared in manuscript.

Place	Date	Hour	Summary of Events and Information	Remarks and references to Appendices
BONDUES AREA	1.12.18 (Sun)		Divine Services were held for all denominations during the morning. A Football Match was played by the Officers in the afternoon, teams finish level.	G.H.
do.	2.12.18 (Mon)		Parades in accordance with the training programme. A lecture on "Exploration" was given by Capt Sharpe R.E. at the "Cirque", Grande Place, TURCOING at 10.30. Educational classes in elementary subjects were commenced 1130 - 1230, also voluntary classes in Shorthand & French were held in the evening. The Lunch Class was well attended. Weather wet.	G.H.
do.	3.12.18 (Tues)		Training in accordance with programme. The C.O. Lt Major Genl. L. & P. Turner C.M.G. D.S.O. inspected Billets during the morning. A number of men attended a Searchlight Tattoo held in the Grande Place, ROUBAIX commencing at 18.00. Two Motor Lorries were provided to convey the men to from ROUBAIX. Weather showery.	G.H.

Original

Army Form C. 2118.

WAR DIARY
or
INTELLIGENCE SUMMARY.
(Erase heading not required.) 29th Battn. Durham Light Infantry

Place	Date	Hour	Summary of Events and Information	Remarks and references to Appendices
BONDUES AREA	4.12.18 (WED)		Men bathed. Several Officers & Men attended 14th Divisional Boxing Competition at the "Cirque" Grande Place, TURCOING during the afternoon. Six entries from this Battalion. Weather showery.	G.H.
do.	5.12.18 (THURS)		Men bathed. A number of Officers & Men attended a Lecture by Mr Harry Dubost in The "Cirque" Grande Place TURCOING at 10.30. Subject "Industrial Peace". 14th Divisional Band Competition was resumed in the afternoon. There were a good attendance of all ranks. Weather fine.	G.H.
do.	6.12.18 (FRI)		Battalion took part in a Divisional Practice of the Army Commanders Inspection by the Army Commander. Recreational training in the afternoon. Weather fine.	G.H.

Original

Army Form C. 2118.

Instructions regarding War Diaries and Intelligence Summaries are contained in F.S. Regs., Part II. and the Staff Manual respectively. Title pages will be prepared in manuscript.

WAR DIARY
or
INTELLIGENCE SUMMARY.
(Erase heading not required.)

29th Battn. Durham Light Infantry

Place	Date	Hour	Summary of Events and Information	Remarks and references to Appendices
BONDUES AREA	6/12/18 (SAT)		C.O. inspected billets. A number of men visited LILLE in view of the visit of His Majesty the King. Recreational training as usual in the afternoon. Weather fine.	G.H.
do	8/12/18 (SUN)		Services were held for all Denominations. Weather fine.	G.H.
do	9/12/18 (MON)		Parades held in accordance with programme. One hours Recreational training in the afternoon. Weather very fine.	G.H.
do	10/12/18 (TUES)		Battalion paraded for inspection of the Divisional Genl. Sir C.R. Woodward K.C.B. K.C.S.I. K.C.M.G. &c. in command of S. Army. Weather showery. 30 Reinforcements reported.	G.H.
do	11/12/18 (WED)		Coys & Battn equipped again for parades in accordance with programme. A number of Officers & Men attended a Lecture by Capt. E.R. Alston in the "Cirque" Grande Place, TURCOING at 14.30. Subject "Flying". Weather showery.	G.H.
do	12/12/18 (THURS)		"A" Coy to Red and Blanket Fumigator. A Lecture was given in the "Cirque" TURCOING at 11.00. Subject "Demobilization". Lecturer Rev. G. Stuttard Kennedy M.C. Weather wet.	G.H.

Original

Instructions regarding War Diaries and Intelligence Summaries are contained in F.S. Regs., Part II. and the Staff Manual respectively. Title pages will be prepared in manuscript.

Army Form C. 2118.

WAR DIARY
or
INTELLIGENCE SUMMARY
(Erase heading not required.) 29. L. Bn. Durham Light Infantry

Place	Date	Hour	Summary of Events and Information	Remarks and references to Appendices
BONDUES AREA	13.12.18 (FRI)		Parades in accordance with programme; one time recreational training in the afternoon. "B" & "D" Coy. bathed, blankets fumigated. 3 men proceeded to England for release &c. Continued weather fine.	G.H.
do.	14.12.18 (SAT)		Kit inspections carried out under Coy. arrangements. H.Q. Coy., Transport, & D.M. Stores bathed, blankets fumigated. A lecture was given by 2n Lt. E.N. Statfield at "The Cirque" TURCOING at 10.30. Subject "Exploration in The Alps", & a number of Officers from attended. Rugby football match played in afternoon 29th D.L.I. v 1/4th Bn. n. Weather fine.	G.H.
do.	15.12.18 (SUN)		Divine services held for all denominations. Officers football match held in the afternoon. Weather fine.	G.H.
do.	16.12.18 (MON)		Training according to programme. football match "D" Coy. v "D" Coy. in the afternoon. Weather fine.	G.H.

Original

Army Form C. 2118.

WAR DIARY
or
INTELLIGENCE SUMMARY

(Erase heading not required.)

Durham Light Infantry 29th Bath.

Place	Date	Hour	Summary of Events and Information	Remarks and references to Appendices
BONDUES	17.12.18 (TUES)		Parades in accordance with instructions circulated. Recreational Training in the afternoon. Weather fine.	G.It.
AREA	18.12.18 (WED)		Training as yesterday. Weather fine.	G.It.
do.	19.12.18 (THURS)		Training as usual. Recreational Training in the afternoon.	G.It.
			Weather fine. Football match played 29th DCLI v 18th DLI.	
do.	20.12.18 (FRI)		Training in accordance with programme. Recreational Training in afternoon. Weather showery.	G.It.
do.	21.12.18 (SAT)		Training as yesterday. Clothing & Arms Field & Kit Inspection. Major F.W.H. Miller M.C. issued Certificates to Major & Co. inspected Boys doomed command.	G.It.
do.	22.12.18 (SUN)		Divine Services were held for all Denominations. Officers Football Match held in the afternoon. Weather showery.	G.It.
do.	23.12.18 (MON)		Training as per programme. Weather fine. A Concert was held in the evening by the Battn. Infant Party in the "Nico" over C. Coy Billets. New Testud at BONDUES Baths.	G.It.

Original.

Army Form C. 2118.

Instructions regarding War Diaries and Intelligence Summaries are contained in F. S. Regs., Part II. and the Staff Manual respectively. Title pages will be prepared in manuscript.

WAR DIARY
or
INTELLIGENCE SUMMARY.
(Erase heading not required.)

29th Batt. Durham Light Infantry

Place	Date	Hour	Summary of Events and Information	Remarks and references to Appendices
BONDUES AREA	24/12/16 (TUES)		Final preparations were made for the Christmas festivities. Weather fine.	G.H.
do	25/12/16 (WED)		Divine Services (voluntary) were held for all Denominations. Christmas Festivities held. A special dinner was served at mid-day consisting of Roast Pork, Apple sauce, Seasoning, Potatoes & Cabbage, Plum Pudding with Rum Sauce, Rum & Coffee. The dinner was thoroughly appreciated, and every man had an ample sufficiency. The C.O. invited the Coy. Sergt. Mess during the progress of the meal. Weather fine.	G.H.
do	26/12/16 (THURS)		No Parades held. Weather fine.	G.H.
do	27/12/16 (FRI)		Training carried out in accordance with instructions circulated to Coys. Recruits Drainage in the afternoon. Weather wet.	G.H.

A6945 Wt. W14432/M1160 350,000 12/16 D. D. & L. Forms/C./2118/14.

Original

Army Form C. 2118.

WAR DIARY
INTELLIGENCE SUMMARY

20th Batt. Durham Light Infantry

(Erase heading not required.)

Instructions regarding War Diaries and Intelligence Summaries are contained in F. S. Regs., Part II. and the Staff Manual respectively. Title pages will be prepared in manuscript.

Place	Date	Hour	Summary of Events and Information	Remarks and references to Appendices
BONDUES	28/12/18 (SAT)		C.O. inspected Kits and Billets. M.O. inspected Coys. Recreational Training as usual in the afternoon. A Concert was given in the evening by the Battalion Concert Party. Weather very wet	G.H.
AREA				
do	29/12/18 (SUN)		Divine Services were held for all Denominations. Weather wet	G.H.
do	30/12/18 (MON)		Training carried out in Lectures from O.C. and Platoon Commanders. Recreational Training in the afternoon. Weather showery	G.H.
do	31/12/18 (TUES)		Training as yesterday. Recreational Training in the afternoon. Weather showery	G.H.

[signature]
Major.
Commanding
20th Batt. Durham Light Infantry

CONFIDENTIAL.

WAR DIARY

- of -

29th Bn., DURHAM LIGHT INFANTRY.

From: 1st January, 1919.
TO: 31st January, 1919.

VOLUME VIII.

Army Form C. 2118.

WAR DIARY
or
INTELLIGENCE SUMMARY.
(Erase heading not required.) Durham Light Infantry 20th Battn.

Place	Date	Hour	Summary of Events and Information	Remarks and references to Appendices
BONDUES AREA	1/1/19 (WED)		Billets were inspected by O.C. Coys. Men were billeted for Bondues. Battalion at BONDUES Church. Recreational Rooms during the evening. A concert was given in the evening by the Battalion Concert Party at the Theatre over Coy Billets. Weather fair.	
do	2/1/19 (THURS)		Training was carried out in Platoon and Company Drill etc. Sports and Voluntary Education Classes were held during the evening. Preparations were made for the move the following day. Weather observed.	
do	3/1/19 (FRI)		Battalion started its march route to TOURCOING area, taking over Billets vacated by the 20th Battn Middlesex Regt. Billets good. Weather observed.	Situation otherwise Sympathetic No. 1
TOURCOING	4/1/19 (SAT)		The Commander of Coys (Major J.K.H. Miller M.C.) inspected kits and Billets. Watching in billets cleaning equipment and quarters. Weather observed.	Sit

Army Form C. 2118.

WAR DIARY
INTELLIGENCE SUMMARY

(Erase heading not required.)

29th Battn Durham Light Infantry

Place	Date	Hour	Summary of Events and Information	Remarks and references to Appendices
TOURCOING	5/10/19	SUN	Divine Service were held for all Denominations. Weather wet	G.H.
do	6/10/19	MON	Training in Platoon and Company Drill, P.D. and Gas Gas. Classes were carried out. Educational Classes in the morning. A Football Match was played in the afternoon 29th D.L.I. v 14th Bn. R.A.M.C. Weather fine	G.H.
do	7/10/19	TUES	Gas hut Training was carried out, and Curriculum Educational Classes held in the morning. Recreational Training in the afternoon. Weather fine.	G.H.
do	8/10/19	WED	Church Parade as yesterday. Compulsory and Voluntary Educational Classes held. Battalion bathed at 14th Divl. Baths, 30 Rue Faidherbe Tourcoing. Pre-Emb. Survey by S.O. inspected billets in the afternoon. Weather fine	G.H.
do	9/10/19	THUR	Training carried out in P.D. Lewis Gun and Arms Drill. Educational Classes as yesterday. Recreational Training in the afternoon. Weather shower.	G.H.

Army Form C. 2118.

WAR DIARY
or
INTELLIGENCE SUMMARY
(Erase heading not required.)

20th Batn Durham Light Infantry

Place	Date	Hour	Summary of Events and Information	Remarks and references to Appendices
TOURCOING	10.1.19 (FRI)		An hour Parade carried out in O.D. Lens Guns & Anne Drill. Educational Classes held in the morning. A lecture was given by Wesleyan Church at the CINEMA HALL, RUE DES ANGES, TOURCOING. Subject "Japanese" Weather fine.	G.F.
do	11.1.19 (SAT)		The Commanding Officer (Capt. & Comdt.) inspected Kits and Billets. Voluntary Educative Classes held. Capt & Comdt & Second in Command Keating Gould 2/Lt F. Goodhead M.C. apologi[zed] have taken in the strength of the Battalion. Divine Services were held for all Denominations.	G.F.
do	12.1.19 (SUN)		Football Match played in the afternoon & Officers 15th L.N.L. v 20th D.L.I. Weather fine. Cold.	G.F.
do	13.1.19 (MON)		Training in O.D. Lens Guns, and Arms Drill was carried out, and Educational Classes held in the morning. Football Match in the afternoon 20th D.L.I. v. Canadians. Weather fine.	G.F.

Army Form C. 2118.

WAR DIARY
INTELLIGENCE SUMMARY
(Erase heading not required.)

20th Battn. Durham Light Infantry

Place	Date	Hour	Summary of Events and Information	Remarks and references to Appendices
TOURCOING	14.1.19 (TUES)		Training was carried out as yesterday. Educational Classes held in the morning and Recreational Training in the afternoon. Weather fine & cold.	Lt.
do	15.1.19 (WED)		One hours Training done and Education Classes held in the morning. Battalion bathed at the 14th Divisional Baths. T.O.E.T. Lt Col. R L Ridley D.S.O. M.C. counted commenced on return from leave. Weather fine.	Lt.
TOURCOING				
do	16.1.19 (THURS)		Training was carried as yesterday, and Education classes held in the morning. Recreational Training in the afternoon. Weather fine.	Lt.
do	17.1.19 (FRI)		Training in Barrack Rooms, in P.T. Lewis Gun and Arms Drill Elementary and Voluntary Education Classes held. Weather fine.	Lt.
do	18.1.19 (SAT)		The Commanding Officer (Lt. Col R L Ridley D.S.O. M.C.) inspected kits and Billets. The Medical Officer inspected Coys. a Football Match was played in the afternoon.	Lt.

29th D.L.I.

Army Form C. 2118.

WAR DIARY
or
INTELLIGENCE SUMMARY
(Erase heading not required.)

29th Battn. Durham Light Infantry

Place	Date	Hour	Summary of Events and Information	Remarks and references to Appendices
TOURCOING	18.1.19 (SAT)		20th D.L.I & 15 D.L.I. Heather fine.	GA
do.	19.1.19 (SUN)		Divine Services were held for all Denominations. Weather fine.	GA
do	20.1.19 (MON)		Training was carried out in P.T. Lewis Gun and Anno Drill. Compulsory & Voluntary Education Classes held. A lecture was given at the Cinema Hall Rue des Anges. Subject "Czecho-Slovaks and Yugo-Slavs". Touring Exhibition was given at the Lycee Boulevard Gambetta. Touring by the American Basket Ball Team.	M
do	21.1.19 (TUES)		Training in P.T. Lewis Gun and Anno Drill. Lewis Gun Officer inspected Guns of all Companies. Compulsory & Voluntary Education classes were held. One hour Recreational Training for the Afternoon. Weather fine.	M
do	22.1.19 (WED)		Training as yesterday. Battalion bathed at the Municipal Baths Tourcoing. Weather fine.	M

Army Form C. 2118.

WAR DIARY
or
INTELLIGENCE SUMMARY.
(Erase heading not required.)

Place	Date	Hour	Summary of Events and Information	Remarks and references to Appendices
TOURCOING	23.1.19 THURS		Training in P.T. Lewis Gun & Arms Drill. Education classes till 12.30 noon. Usual Recreational Training in afternoon.	MH
	24.1.19 FRI		Rehearsal for presentation of colours at 5.19. 6.55. Usual training carried out by remainder of the battalion. Weather fine.	
			Two officers & 180 O.R. proceeded to Lille to witness performance at the Nouveaux Theatre. Weather fine.	MH
	25.1.19 SAT		Lt Gen Sir B de Lisle, 5th Army Commander presented colours to the Battalion in the GRAND PLACE, ROUBAIX. Weather fine.	MH
	26.1.19 SUN		Divine Service was held for all Denominations. Weather fine.	MH
	27.1.19 MON		Training was carried out in P.T. Lewis Gun & Arms Drill. Compulsory & Voluntary Education classes were held. Weather — slight snowfall.	MH
	28.1.19 TUES		Training as yesterday. Weather — some snow fell.	MH
	29.1.19 WED		Training in Lewis Gun Arms Drill & P.T. Weather fine.	MH
	30.1.19 THURS		Training was carried out in P.T. Lewis Gun & Arms Drill. Compulsory & Voluntary Education was carried on from the morning. Weather fine.	MH

Army Form C. 2118.

WAR DIARY
or
INTELLIGENCE SUMMARY.
(Erase heading not required.)

Instructions regarding War Diaries and Intelligence Summaries are contained in F. S. Regs., Part II. and the Staff Manual respectively. Title pages will be prepared in manuscript.

Place	Date	Hour	Summary of Events and Information	Remarks and references to Appendices
TOURCOING	31/1/19 FRI.		Training in arms Drill, P.T., Lewis Gun, Education classes (Compulsory & Voluntary) and box Respirator training in the afternoon. Weather fine.	

R.W. Ridley Lieut-Colonel
Commanding 24th Durham Light Infantry

C O N F I D E N T I A L.

W A R D I A R Y

- of -

29th Bn., DURHAM LIGHT INFANTRY.

From: 1st February, 1919.
To: 28th February, 1919.

VOLUME IX.

Army Form C. 2118.

WAR DIARY
or
INTELLIGENCE SUMMARY.
(Erase heading not required.)

Instructions regarding War Diaries and Intelligence Summaries are contained in F. S. Regs., Part II. and the Staff Manual respectively. Title pages will be prepared in manuscript.

Place	Date	Hour	Summary of Events and Information	Remarks and references to Appendices
TOURCOING	1.2.19 SAT		The Commanding Officer (Lt-Col R.W. Ridley DSO MC) inspected billets. The I.O.C, Hick Infantry Brigade gave a lecture to the Battalion on "Murdering the Peace". Weather fine.	
	2.2.19 SUN		Divine Service was held for all Denominations. Weather fine.	JR
	3.2.19 MON		Training was carried out in Lewis Drill, P.T. Lewis Gun Compulsory & Voluntary Education Schools held. Weather fine.	JR
	4.2.19 TUES		Training in P.T. Lewis Drill, Lewis Gun Compulsory & Voluntary Education Classes. Also house Recreational Training in the afternoon. Weather fine.	JR
	5.2.19 WED		Training as yesterday. Battalion bathed at the Municipal Baths. Young Snowfall in evening.	JR
	6.2.19 THURS		Tourcoing. Training in Lewis Gun, P.T. & Lewis Drill. Weather fine.	JR
	7.2.19 FRI		Training as yesterday. Weather fine.	JR
	8.2.19 SAT		The Commanding Officer (Lt Col R.W. Ridley DSO MC) delivered a lecture on "Advantages & Disadvantages of Re-enlisting in Army". Weather fine.	JR

A6945 Wt. W14422/M1160 350,000 12/16 D.D.&L. Forms/C./2118/14.

Army Form C. 2118.

WAR DIARY
or
INTELLIGENCE SUMMARY.
(Erase heading not required.) Durham Light Infantry

Instructions regarding War Diaries and Intelligence Summaries are contained in F. S. Regs., Part II. and the Staff Manual respectively. Title pages will be prepared in manuscript. 2/9th Battn.

Place	Date	Hour	Summary of Events and Information	Remarks and references to Appendices
TOURCOING	9.2.19	SUN	Divine Service was held for all Denominations. Weather fine	M
	10.2.19	MON	One hours training in P.T. Lewis Gun & Arms Drill. Lecturers & Musketry Education classes held. Weather fine	M
	11.2.19	TUES	Training & Education as yesterday. Weather fine	M
	12.2.19	WED	Training was carried on in Barrack Rooms & Lewis Gun. P.T. & Arms Drill. Education classes held. Weather fine.	M
	13.2.19	THURS	Training as yesterday. Weather fine	M
	14.2.19	FRI	Training in Lewis Gun. P.T. & Arms Drill. Weather fine	M
	15.2.19	SAT	Training in Lewis Gun and P.T. in Barrack Rooms also Educational Classes. Weather fine.	9./Am.
	16.2.19	SUN	Divine Service was held for all denominations. Weather Wet.	9 p.m.
	17.2.19	MON	Training in Lewis Gun and P.T. carried out in Barrack Rooms. Educational Classes and Recreational Training. Weather Fine.	9 p.m.
	18.2.19	TUES	Lewis Gun. P.T. & Educational Training carried out. Weather Wet	9 p.m.
	19.2.19	WED	Training as yesterday. Weather Wet.	9 p.m.
	20.2.19	THURS	Training as usual in Barrack Rooms. Half the Battn went to the Theatre at night. Weather wet	9 p.m.

WAR DIARY
INTELLIGENCE SUMMARY.

(Erase heading not required.) Durham Light Infantry

Army Form C. 2118.

Place	Date	Hour	Summary of Events and Information	Remarks and references to Appendices
Tourcoing	21.2.19 FRI		Training in Lewis Gun & P.T. carried out in Barrack Rooms. Educational Classes. The other half of Battn went to the Theatre Municipal at night. Weather Wet	9M.
	22.2.19 SAT		A general kit inspection was carried out by O.C. Coys. Weather wet	9M.
	23.2.19 SUN		Divine Service held for all denominations. Weather wet	9M.
	24.2.19 MON		Training in Lewis Gun & P.T. carried out in Barrack Rooms. Weather fine	9M.
	25.2.19 TUES		Parade the same as usual. Weather fine	9M.
	26.2.19 WED		One hours training in Lewis Gun and P.T. carried out in Barrack Rooms. Compulsory Educational Classes. Weather fine	9M.
	27.2.19 THUR		Lewis Gun & P.T. Training carried out in Barrack Rooms. Educational Classes. Weather fine	9M.
	28.2.19 FRI		Final inspections and preparations made for the departure of men in the Battn eligible for Army of Occupation. Weather fair	9M.

Rev Ridley
Lieut. Colonel
Commanding 29" Bn Durham Light Infantry

Appendix No. 1

S E C R E T.   Copy No. 6

29th. Bn. The DURHAM LIGHT INFANTRY.

OPERATION ORDER NO 34.

Refce Map Sheet 36 – 1/40,000.

(1) The Battalion will move by route march to-morrow, Jany 3rd, to the TOURCOING Area.

(2) Head of the column will be at Cross-roads F.7.d.4.7. at 10.05 hrs.
Order of march will be :– H.Q. Coy, 'A', 'B', 'C', and 'D' Coys – Transport.
Route will be from cross-roads F.7.d.4.7. to cross-roads F.14.a.5.6. and thence to destination.
100 yards distance will be maintained between Companies and Transport.
25 yards will be left between each group of 6 vehicles.
Dress :– 'Full Marching Order' (less haversack and greatcoat). Caps S.D. Jerkins in pack, steel helmets outside the pack.

(3) Billets will be taken over from 20th. Bn. Middlesex Regt.

(4) O.C. 'D' Coy will provide stragglers party of 1 Officer and 6 Other Ranks.

(5) O.C. 'A' Coy will detail party of 1 Officer and 1 Platoon to act as rear party. Each company will send 1 man who knows location of his Company billets, to report to above Officer at 08.30 hrs. This Officer will obtain Clearing Certificate in duplicate from Representative of 20th. Bn. Middlesex Regt and forward to Battn. H.Q. immediately on arrival in new area.
Each Company will obtain 'Certificat de bien vivre' for each billet.

(6) Advance party has proceeded to-day.

(7) All Officers' Valises, blankets, sandbags, Coy Boxes etc., will be stacked on main road near Coy H.Q. by 08.00 hrs.
3 lorries are expected to report at Battn. H.Q. at 08.00 hrs
Q.M. will detail guide to report at Battn H.Q. at 07.45 hrs.
Lorries will do 2 or more journeys if necessary.

(8) Q.M. will arrange to hand over the following Stores to Representative of 20th. Bn. Middlesex Regt :–
Beds, Washing bowls, Forms, palliasses, Latrines, Tables, Ablution benches, Latrine buckets.
Similar stores will be taken over from 20th. Bn. Middlesex Regt.
All component parts of Adrian and Standard Huts will be handed over.

(9) Receipts for all stores handed over will be obtained in duplicate by Q.M. and forwarded to Battn H.Q. by the 4th inst., together with List in duplicate of stores taken over in the TOURCOING Area.

(10) In view of the nature of the buildings occupied as billets in the TOURCOING Area special attention is to be paid to ensuring that all fire orders are complied with. Copies of Fire Orders for the Brigade Area in TOURCOING are attached. (Issued to O.C. Coys, H.Q. Coy, T.O. Q.M.)

(11) Arrival in billets and falling out certificates will be notified to Battn. H.Q. immediately.

(12) ACKNOWLEDGE.

F.W.Pepper
2/Lieut & A/Adjutant,
29th. Bn. Durham Light Infantry.

3.1.19.
Issued at 19.00 hrs.
Copies to :-

No. 1. C.O.
No. 2. O.C. 'A' Coy.
No. 3. O.C. 'B' Coy.
No. 4. O.C. 'C' Coy.
No. 5. O.C. 'D' Coy.
No. 6. O.C. H.Q. Coy.
No. 7. 41st Inf Bde.
No. 8. T.O.
No. 9. Q.M.
No. 10. 2/Lt. R.V. Atkins.
No. 11. Area Commdt, DONDUES.
No. 12. 20th Middlesex Regt.
No. 13. War Diary.
No. 14. do
No. 15. File.

CONFIDENTIAL.

WAR DIARY

- of -

29th DURHAM LIGHT INFANTRY.

From: 1st March, 1919.
To: 31st March, 1919.

VOLUME X.

WAR DIARY
or
INTELLIGENCE SUMMARY

(Erase heading not required.)

Army Form C. 2118.

Place	Date	Hour	Summary of Events and Information	Remarks and references to Appendices
TOURS en 19	MAR 1st SAT		Reveille at 4 am and for Army of Occupation proceeded by train at 7.30 am to the 2/6 Durham Light Infantry, the B.G.C. and all Batn. Officers were present. Weather fine.	9p.m.
	2.3.19 SUN		Voluntary Service were held for the men that were were left. Weather fine	9p.m.
	3.3.19 MON		Having no men on parade only ordinary fatigues were carried out. Weather wet.	9p.m. 9p.m.
	4.3.19 TUES		Men in billets and usual fatigues for the Baths	9p.m.
	9.3.19 SAT		All available Inoculation stores were moved to ESTAIMPUIS forming a "Brigade Group Dump"	a/On
	9.3.19 to 31.3.19		From 9.3.19 until 31.3.19 Men were in Billets at the same place. All spare Officers were demobilized on the usual Weather variable with frequent falls of snow.	9p.m.

P.W. Ridley Lieut Col Commanding
29 Bn. Durham Light Infantry

CONFIDENTIAL.

WAR DIARY

- of -

29th Bn., DURHAM LIGHT INFANTRY.

From: 1st April, 1919.
To: 30th April, 1919.

VOLUME XI.

Army Form C. 2118.

WAR DIARY
or
INTELLIGENCE SUMMARY.
(Erase heading not required.) Durham Light Infantry

Instructions regarding War Diaries and Intelligence Summaries are contained in F. S. Regs., Part II. and the Staff Manual respectively. Title pages will be prepared in manuscript. 9 9 Bn.

Place	Date	Hour	Summary of Events and Information	Remarks and references to Appendices
Tourcoing	Apr 1st to 30		The Battn. came in billets at Tourcoing during the month, no special work or any matter of interest took place during this ——— period. The weather during the first half of the month was very fine and warm, the latter was very cold wet snow and Rain.	9/9n

J.P.K. Jeffrey Capt for Lieut Col

Commanding 29th Bn. Durham Light Infty

www.ingramcontent.com/pod-product-compliance
Lightning Source LLC
Chambersburg PA
CBHW081425160426
43193CB00013B/2198